Light from Darkness

Light from Darkness

Samael Aun Weor

GLORIAN

Light from Darkness
A Glorian Book / 2023

Originally published in Spanish as "El Collar del Buddha: Mensaje de Navidad 1966 - 1967"

Print ISBN 978-1-943358-19-9

Glorian Publishing is a non-profit organization. All proceeds further the distribution of these books. For more information, visit glorian.org

Contents

Illustrations

Chapter 1

The Sun Child

Most beloved Gnostic brothers and sisters,

On this night in which we jubilantly celebrate the Christmas Eve of 1966, it is essential to very thoroughly study the mysteries of Christ.[1]

At the dawning of the great cosmic day, the First Logos,[2] the Father, said to the Third Logos, the Holy Spirit, "Go, fertilize my spouse, the chaotic matter, the Great Mother, so that life can arise; look into it." Thus, this is how the Father spoke, and the Third Logos reverently bowed, at the dawning of the aurora of creation.

The cosmocreators, the army of builders of the dawn, the host of the Elohim,[3] the Third Logos, worked in the seven temples of the chaos.[4]

Three forces are indispensable for all creation: the positive force, the negative force, and the neutral force.[5] Before the altar of the temple, one Elohim polarized the masculine, positive force of his Self, and another the feminine, negative force of her Self. While on the ground floor of the temple, a choir of Elohim represented the neutral force. Thus, in this manner, the order of the three forces was established in each of the seven temples of the primeval chaos. The Divine Male chanted, the Divine Female chanted, the choir of Elohim chanted. The entire liturgy of the seven temples was chanted. Thus, this is how the Great Word made the womb of the Great Divine Mother fecund.

---

1 The Cosmic Christ is a force, as electricity or gravity are. See glossary.

2 Logos (Greek λόγος "word") refers to a manifested deity, as a word is the manifestation of a thought. See glossary. Here, the three logoi relate to the fundamental trinity / trimurti, the law of three.

3 Hebrew, a plural word that simultaneously means a single god-goddess and multiple gods and goddesses. See glossary.

4 Greek χάος khaos, the primitive state of the universe, from which occurs creation (Genesis).

5 The law of three, symbolized by the trinity of gods in each religion.

An Egyptian representation of the Sun Child with the Divine Mother

> *"In the beginning was the Word [First Logos], and the Word [Second Logos] was with God, and the Word [Third Logos] was God. The same was in the beginning with God. All things were made by him; and without him was not any thing made that was made. In him was life; and the life was the light of men..."* –John 1:1-4

The Word made the waters of life fecund; thus, this is how the universe in its germinal state splendidly arose at the aurora.

The Holy Spirit fecundated the Great Mother, and the Christ was born. The Second Logos is always the child of the Virgin Mother. She is always virgin before childbirth, during childbirth, and after childbirth. She is Maria, Isis, Adonia, Insobertha, Rhea, Cybele, etc. She is the primeval chaos, the primordial substance, the raw matter of the Great Work.

The Cosmic Christ is the army of the Great Word, is always born in the worlds, and is crucified in each one of them so that all beings can have life and have it in abundance.

My brothers and sisters: observe the King Star in its elliptical movement [see illustration, next page] . The sun moves from south to north and from north to south. The birth of

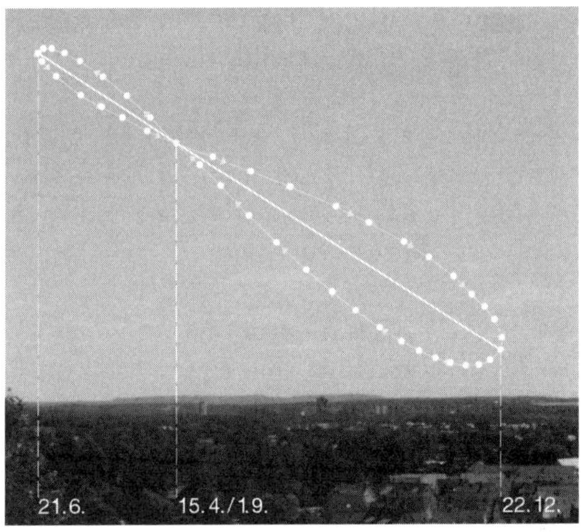

An illustration of an analemma pattern of the position of the sun, if photographed once a week for a year.

the Sun Child is celebrated when the Sun advances towards the north. The Sun Child is born the twenty-fourth of December at midnight in order to dawn on the twenty-fifth.

If the Sun Christ did not advance towards the north, the entire Earth would become a great mass of ice and all life would perish, therefore from the twenty-fourth of December the Sun God advances towards the north in order to animate, give heat and life to all creatures.

The Sun Child is born the twenty-fourth of December in order to dawn on the twenty-fifth, and is crucified in the spring equinox in order to give life to everything that exists.

The fixed date of its birth and the variable date of its death always have a deep significance within all the religious theologies.

The Sun Child is born weak and needy in this humble manger of the world and in one those very long nights of winter, where the days are very short in the regions of the north.

During the time of Christmas, the sign of the Celestial Virgin rises on the horizon, and thus this is how the child is born in order to save to the world.

During his infancy, the Sun Christ is surrounded by dangers, since by all means it is very clear that during the first days the kingdom of darkness is much longer than light—his kingdom—yet despite all the terrible dangers that threaten him, he survives.

Time passes... the days cruelly are extended, and finally the spring equinox—Easter, the Holy Week—arrives, which is the moment in which he has to cross from one end to the other—that is, the moment of the crucifixion of the Lord on this our world.

The Sun Christ crucifies himself on our planet Earth in order to give life to everything that exists. After his death he resurrects within all creation in order to ripen the grape and every grain. The law of the Logos is sacrifice.

This is the cosmic drama that is repeated from moment to moment throughout the infinite space, in all of the worlds, in all of the suns. This is the cosmic drama that is represented in all the temples of Egypt, Greece, India, Mexico, etc. This is the cosmic drama that is represented in all the temples of all of the worlds of the infinite space.

The second aspect of this great cosmic drama corresponds with complete exactitude to any sacred individual who by means of the revolution of the consciousness attains the Venustic Initiation and therefore becomes a solar hero...

Chapter 2

The Milky Way

Christmas is a solar festivity, an ineffable cosmic festivity, whose origin is found within the profound night of time.

The three dimensional physical sun is only a vehicle of action of the spiritual sun. Beyond the physical sun, the mystic finds the Sun of Midnight, the Star of Bethlehem, the Cosmic Christ.

All the archaic religions always rendered cult to the Sun, thus even the Vatican is built in such a manner so that its doors are open towards the East, towards where the Sun rises.

Primeval Christians always said with great devotion, "Our Lord Jesus Christ, the Sun."

The motion of the King Star amongst the innumerable stars of the infinite space and in relation to the nearest worlds is astounding; it moves at a speed of twenty kilometers per second.

Within the interior of the Milky Way, the Sun rotates at an amazing speed; it moves it at a rate of 270 kilometers per second. In its movement, the Sun drags the Earth and the entire solar system.

The planet Earth on which we live, move, and have our Being is something more than a mass of matter; beyond any doubt, it is a living organism upon whose epidermis we all live as simple parasites.

The path tread by the planet Earth throughout the infinite space is very complicated and difficult.

Indeed, the planet Earth dancing around the sun amongst the music of the spheres travels at a vertiginous speed rotating along the interior of this formidable galaxy in which we live.

Indeed, the Milky Way is so gigantic that even though the Sun is traveling at 270 kilometers per second, it will take about 200 million years to circle completely around it.

The Milky Way is a living, cosmic organism, a spiral-like body within which is our solar system.

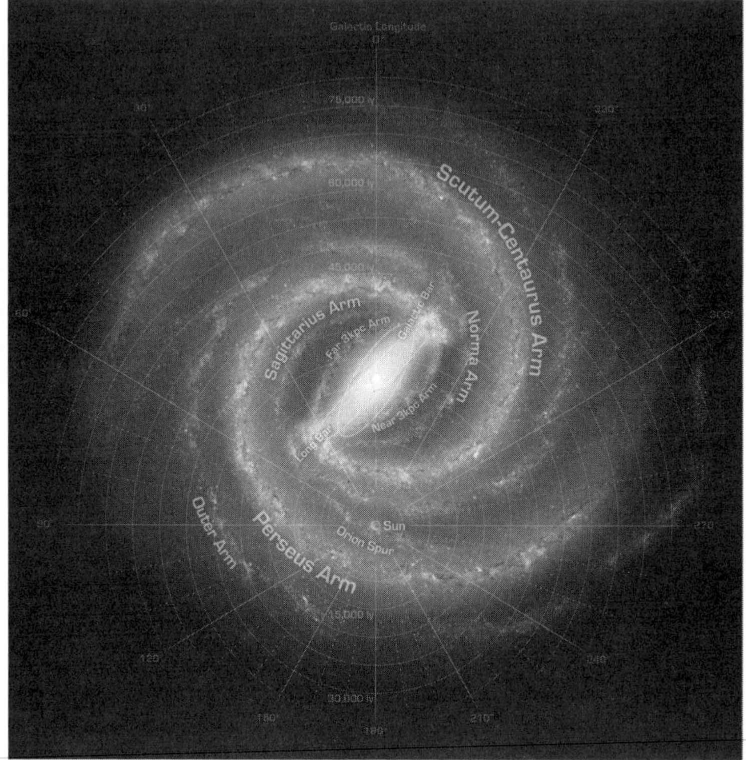

THE MILKY WAY GALAXY

Any galaxy, including our Milky Way, has in fact and by its own right the same fundamental design.

Three forces are processed within any galaxy:

- first, the centripetal
- second, the centrifugal
- third, the neutral, that serves as a point of support and equilibrium

The centrifugal force provides the galaxy with a spiral type of movement, similar to a whirlwind over sandy ground that provides spiral movement to the dust column that it raises.

The Milky Way, with about eighteen million suns and innumerable planets and moons, has the Central Sun Sirius as its gravitational center.

Ancient esoteric traditions affirm that the Transcended Church is in the Central Sun Sirius.

Inside the temple of Sirius, adepts[6] can have the joy of encountering the disciples of the God Sirius.

When some adept tries to go beyond the Milky Way, he is always forced to go back to Sirius. It is prohibited for the adepts of the planet Earth to go beyond Sirius.

Astronomers know very well that beyond the Milky Way there are only three visible galaxies that can be seen by the naked eye, without the aid of a telescope. Two of them can be seen from the southern hemisphere; these are the Great and Small Magellanic Clouds, named in honor of Ferdinand Magellan, the famous Portuguese explorer.

When they go beyond Sirius, the adepts of the great White Lodge[7] can see two world orders that glitter wonderfully with a beautiful pink color; in those two galaxies are other types of cosmic laws unknown to the inhabitants of the Milky Way.

In the sacred texts of esoteric wisdom there is a maxim that states, "Where the light shines more brightly, there too the darkness is more dense."

Within the superior worlds[8] any adept can verify that next to a temple of light there is in contrast a temple of frightful darkness. Thus, based on this rule, we can assure without fear of being mistaken that the Central Sun Sirius is a binary star, and that its companion is a gigantic tenebrous world.

---

6 (Latin) adeptus, "One who has obtained." In esotericism, a title earned through internal initiations. "...whosoever reaches the fifth Initiation of the Fire [Tiphereth] becomes an adept..." –Samael Aun Weor, *Tarot and Kabbalah*

7 The ancient collection of pure human beings who uphold and propagate the highest and most sacred of sciences. It is called "white" due to its purity and cleanliness (ie. the absence of pride, lust, anger, etc.). This "brotherhood" or "lodge" includes men and women of the highest order from every race, culture, creed and religion.

8 Aspects of nature that vibrate at higher frequencies than we can perceive with our physical senses. Classically, the superior worlds are called "heavens, nirvana," etc. "Whosoever wants to awaken the consciousness in the Superior Worlds must begin by awakening it in the here and now." –Samael Aun Weor, *Fundamentals of Gnostic Education*

The cosmic forces that govern the Supra / Heaven come to the planet Earth from Sirius, while the forces that govern the Infra / Inferno descend to us from its tenebrous brother. Among astronomers Sirius is known colloquially as the "Dog Star," and its tenebrous companion as "the Pup."

Our galaxy is gigantic, wonderful, astounding. Our galaxy measures about 100,000 light years in diameter and about 10,000 light years in thickness.

The Sun that warms us and give us life—our beloved Sun, source of all life—is located about 3,000 light years from the center, which places it a third of the distance between the center of the galaxy and one of its borders; it seems that it is near to the inner ring of a spiral arm, and also to a very weak and distant group of stars and to another group of stars nearer to the center.

There are many thousands and millions of galaxies in the infinite space. It is estimated that in a space of about 250,000,000 of light years, there are around 2,000,000,000 galaxies, and even for this very tremendous distance there is no indication of a limit.

The situation of our solar system is, beyond any doubt and without any exaggeration, similar to a blood cell within the human body.

Under a microscope we can verify that a white corpuscle is also made up of a nucleus or Sun (its cytoplasm or sphere of influence); this nucleus is also surrounded all around by millions of systems or similar cells, which together form a great Being whose nature would be inconceivable to such a cell.

The Milky Way is a living organism that was born in the ninth sphere[9] from the water and the fire.

Those who suppose that the galaxies, including the Milky Way, had their origin in the [big bang theory] explosion of some primitive atom are very mistaken.

There is an esoteric principle that states, "That which is above is like that which is below."

---

9 In Kabbalah, a reference to the sephirah Yesod of the Tree of Life. When you place the Tree of Life over your body, Yesod is related to your sexual organs.

If the origin of this small microcosmic galaxy called human being had its origin in the ninth sphere—sex—then without fear of misleading ourselves we can logically deduce that the origin of our galaxy and of all the galaxies of the infinite has to be sought within the ninth sphere, sex.

The temple of wisdom is found in the ninth sphere; the temple of wisdom is located between the phallus and the uterus.

By all means, it is impossible to experience the truth about the origin of the galaxies if we do not enter into the ninth sphere (sex).

In the dawning of life, the sexual connubium of the word makes the waters of the Chaos fecund. This is how the galaxies are born and this is how the worlds are born.

The sexual fire of the Kundalini[10] always makes the belly of the Great Mother fecund.

> *"In the beginning was the Word."*

10 Sanskrit कुण्डलिनी, also called Shekinah (Hebrew שכינה), Pentecost, etc. The power of the Divine Mother that awakens in those who earn it.

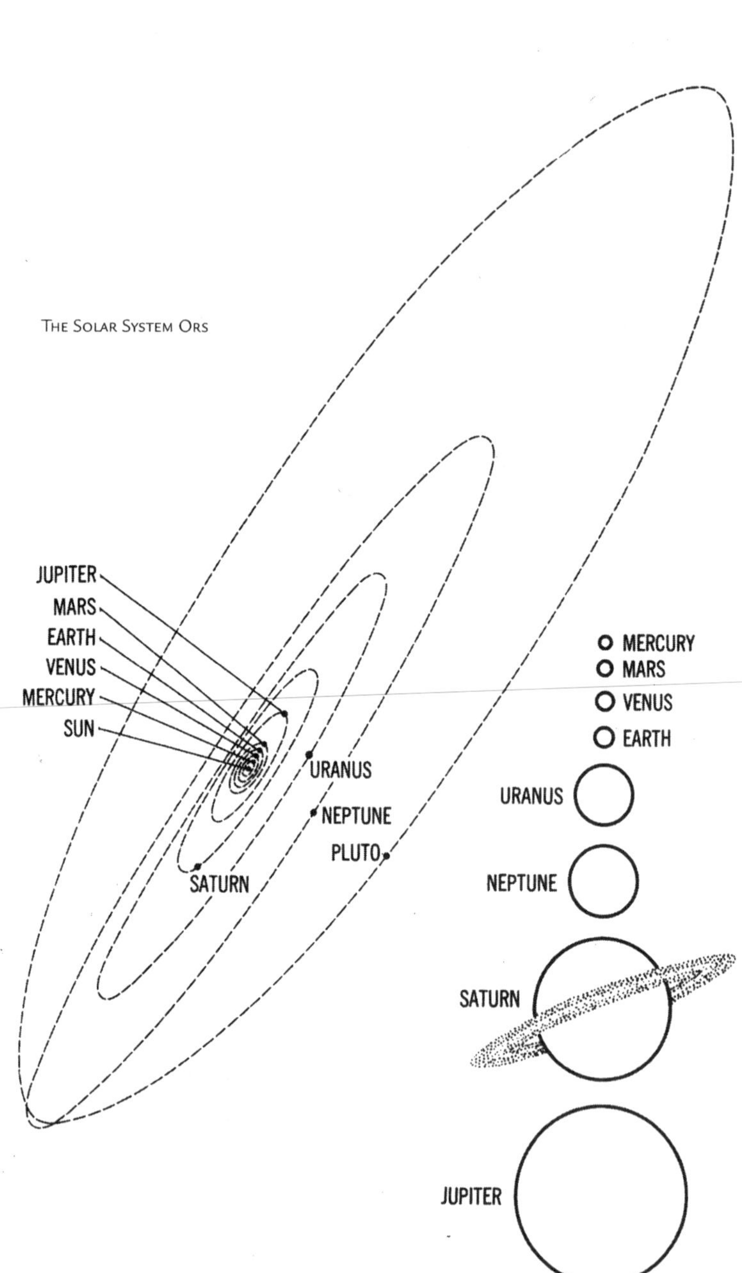
The Solar System Ors
JUPITER
MARS
EARTH
VENUS
MERCURY
SUN
URANUS
NEPTUNE
PLUTO
SATURN
MERCURY
MARS
VENUS
EARTH
URANUS
NEPTUNE
SATURN
JUPITER

Chapter 3

The Solar System Ors

In Nirvana, the significance of family, tribe, clan, has disappeared, since all the beings there consider themselves equal members of a great family. Variety is unity. Nevertheless, all of us, the brothers and sisters, have been able to verify by means of observation and experience that there is a sort of family in each one of the groups of Elohim or Prajapatis[11] who govern the different solar systems of this galaxy in which we live. The sense of cosmic association amongst each group of Elohim makes of them something like ineffable, divine, sublime families.

So, the cosmic family who governs our solar system of Ors in which we live, move and have our Being, has amongst its more distinguished members Gabriel, Raphael, Uriel, Michael, Samael, Zachariel, and Oriphiel. Each of these mentioned brethren is a chief of angelical hosts; each of these brethren has to work intensely in the Great Work of the Father.

Gabriel is the regent of the Moon. Raphael is the regent of Mercury. Uriel governs Venus. Michael is the king of the Sun. Samael is the regent of Mars. Zachariel is the leader of Jupiter. And Orifiel governs the destinies of ancient Saturn, the elder of the heavens.

11 Sanskrit "lords of procreation;" refers to any divinity who creates life.

The Classical Order of the Seven Planetary Angels

Each regent genie[12] is the indweller of a cosmic temple, a planetary temple, which is always found in the core of each sphere, of each planet.

In the astral body,[13] any master of the White Lodge can visit the heart temple of the planet Earth. The genie of the Earth is the one the Bible refers to as Melchizedek, Changam, the king of the world.

It has been said to us that the genie of the Earth has a physical body similar to ours, yet eternal, immortal. Some Lamas from Tibet have had the great joy of having met Changam personally.

The genie of the Earth lives in the subterranean kingdom of Agartha in company of the initiate survivors of Lemuria[14] and Atlantis.[15] The race of Agartha only waits for the degenerate Aryan root race[16] that presently lives upon the surface of the Earth to perish by fire.

When all of us—the perverse ones of this root race—have perished, then they, the survivors of Lemuria and Atlantis, will mix with some select survivors from our present Aryan root race and will repopulate the Earth; they will originate the future sixth root race.

Within the interior of the Earth there are Lemurian and Atlantean survivors with physical bodies; these races possess all the scientific atomic inventions of ancient times.

The king of the world works intensely, and in his work is assisted by the Goros; these are great beings who govern life and death in all of the planes of cosmic consciousness.

The Earth is a living organism that spins around the Sun. The planetary genie keeps it firm in its march. The Earth is one of the members of the great cosmic family of the solar system of Ors. All the sidereal bodies next to this Earth—gov-

12 From Semitic root JNN, literally, 'beings that are concealed from the senses'

13 The body created in the third initiation of Major Mysteries, which is related to the fifth dimension, the emotional center, and to the sephirah Hod.

14 The third root race of this planet.

15 The fourth root race of this planet.

16 The fifth and current root race of this planet.

erned by Melchizedek, king of fire—comprise this complicated family.

Many varied objects are held in the bosom of the solar system of Ors. Nine known planets—governed by indescribable beings—orbit around the sun Ors, along with thirty-one known satellites, thousands of asteroids, comets, and many millions of meteoric particles. Although it seems incredible, and in spite of their number and of the enormous cosmic mass that all these bodies represent, more of the 99 percent of the matter of the solar system of Ors is totally concentered around the Sun.

Indeed, the king star is the heart of the solar system of Ors. The seven Chohans[17]—who direct the seven great cosmic rays—live and work within the temple heart of the Sun, located in the center of that radiating sphere.

Few are the human beings of the planet Earth who can visit the temple heart of the Sun in their astral bodies.

A tremendous and frightful precipice leads the initiate to the vestibule of wisdom. Anyone who arrives at the sacred threshold must reverently prostrate himself before the guardian of the temple. A narrow path leads the visitant to the temple heart, where the seven Chohans dwell, terrifically.

The entire life of the solar system of Ors intensely palpitates in the heart of the Sun. The gravitational force of the Sun maintains the entire solar family within their mechanical orbits. All of the mechanics of the solar system of Ors march in accordance with the great law. The orbits concentrated in the planets—that dancingly spin around the sun, amidst the great symphonies of the cosmic diapason—are wisely related in accordance with Bode's Law.[18] When taking the geometrical development 0, 3, 6, 12, 24, 48, 96, 192, and adding 4 to each number, we obtain a series that more or less represents the distances between the planetary orbits and the Sun. Mercury—the lord of science, the messenger of the gods—moves around the Sun with a vertiginous speed. Venus the star of music, love and beauty, second in relation to the Sun, moves a lit-

17 "Lord, Master"

18 Approximate relative distances of most of the planets.

tle slower; and the Earth, our wretched, forlorn, and martyred Earth, that is third, moves under the wise direction of Changam or Melchizedek, in a yet slower manner.

Our beloved solar system of Ors neighbors a solar system named Baleaooto. The famous comet Solni in its orbit at times comes dangerously close to the shining sun Baleaooto, which is thereby forced to increase a very strong electrical tension in order to firmly maintain its habitual cosmic path. As is very natural and logical, this tension provokes the same identical tension in all the neighboring suns, among which is our Sun named Ors. This is the law of Solioonensius, that also affects the planets that rotate around their corresponding suns. The Earth cannot be an exception to this law of Solioonensius. The terrible electrical tension brings about bloody revolutions and frightful catastrophes.

In the ancient Egypt of the Pharaohs, Solioonensius manifested twice. In the first, the crowds in bloody revolution chose new governors by means of blood and death. They removed the eyes from all the governors of the ruling class. In the second manifestation of this cosmic law, the Egyptian crowds, frightfully infuriated, rose against their governors and killed them by skewering the body of each one of them with a sacred metal cable; this cable was dragged down and thrown into the river Nile. This novel "skewer" seemed rather like a gigantic, macabre necklace.

The Bolshevik revolution was also the outcome of a Solioonensius.

In the past, whenever the law of the Solioonensius manifested, there were great social catastrophes. Nonetheless, the comprehensive populaces take advantage of the law of the Solioonensius in order to enter the path of inner realization.

Seen from afar, the solar system of Ors looks like a man walking through the unalterable infinite. Let us understand that the perception-moment of that comparable being—by one who contemplates the path of the Sun—is eighty years. Astronomers affirm that our solar system Ors travels towards the star Vega at the rate of twenty kilometers per second. The concrete fact is that in eighty years, the sun, leaving behind itself all the shining radiation of its wonderful system, victoriously advances in the sacred space approximately 50,000,000,000 km (fifty billion kilometers). The sphere of radiation, the fire band, or the long and shining body of our solar system—in eighty years—is a figure five times longer than wide, and beautifully proportioned like a standing human body.

The attraction exerted by the Sun governs all the movements of the solar family. Thus, it is clear that the nearer the planets are, the greater their speed must be, in order to energetically resist the tremendous force of solar attraction.

The planets that compose the cosmic solar family vary in size, growing generally from the smallest—the quick Mercury, the messenger of the Gods, who is the nearest to the center—until the powerful thundering Jupiter, the father of all the gods, which is at the middle of the distance between the center and the circumference, and thereafter the sizes of the planets diminish again to the most external well-known planet Pluto, which is a bit larger than quick Mercury.

After many years of observation and experience, it has been possible to verify, beyond any doubt, that the more remote the planets are, the slower their speeds are around the Christ Sun; indeed their speeds diminish from the fifty kilometers per second of Mercury, to the five of Neptune, the lord of occult wisdom, the king of the sea.

The axis of the solar system of Ors—that is to say, the Sun itself—performs its rotation around an interstellar magnetic center or cosmic chakra. That rotation is performed in one month. Quick Mercury, the celestial messenger, performs its rotation around the king star in three months. Venus performs its dance around the Sun in eight months. The Earth performs its voyage around the Sun in twelve months. The marvelous dance of Neptune the king of the sea, around the Sun, is of one hundred sixty and four years.

The cosmic figure of the solar system of Ors is extraordinarily complex and beautiful.

The planetary pieces, transformed into multiple spirals of several tensions and diameters, resemble a shining series of divine coverings that dim the long hot and white filament of the Sun Ors. Each one magnificently radiates its own characteristic heat and brightness; this marvelous combined conjunction is like a mysterious and sublime fabric, spiderweb net, splendidly woven with the multiple, eccentric trajectories of thousands of asteroids and long-tailed comets, glowing with fire breath and jingling with a subtle and incredibly harmonious music, based totally on the three compasses of the mahavan [large rhythm] and chotavan [small rhythm] that sustain the universe firmly in its march.

Indeed, the solar system of Ors is a living cosmic creature who was born many millions years ago in the ninth sphere (sex). All human beings are similar in design and constitution—likewise happens to all the suns of the infinite space.

What makes a distinction amongst humans, these from the others, is their degree of consciousness. What makes a distinction amongst the suns is their degree of radiation. In their depths, light and consciousness are one, same phenomenon. Light and consciousness obey the same laws, increasing or decreasing exactly in the same manner.

The cosmic design of humans and Suns is found in the Chaos, within the universal sperm.[19]

The self-development of the Kosmos Human, or of the solar system, the enlightenment and gradual irradiation of one or the other, are the degree of self-generated consciousness of any solar cosmos, or any Kosmos Human. It totally depends on the same individual being.

In order for a human being to become totally cognizant of one's Self, all of one's parts must become totally cognizant of themselves.

In order for a Sun to become totally radiant, then all of its planets—its cosmic organs—must become totally radiant.

The task of any universe and any being, from the gigantic sun to the insignificant cell, is to awaken consciousness.

---

19 From Ancient Greek σπέρμα (spérma) literally means "that which is sown," and is used for "the seed of plants, also of animals." Since to grow human beings the seeds of both sexes are required, the word sperm or semen actually means the sexual seed of both males and females.

The solar system of Ors will become more radiant as each of its worlds, each person, each living cell, is awakening consciousness.

All the human beings of the planet Earth have their consciousness asleep. It is impossible to experience that which is the Truth while the consciousness is totally asleep.

There are four states of consciousness:

First: dreaming during the vigil state.

Second: dreaming during those moments in which the physical body is sleeping.

Third: self-cognizance.

Fourth: awakened, objective consciousness.

Normally, people live in the first two states of consciousness. Yes, people not only dream when the physical body is resting, but people also continue dreaming in the wrongly named "vigil" state.

It is very rare is to find a human being with cognizance. Yet, sadly, people firmly believe that they have their consciousnesses already awakened.

It is impossible to arrive at objective knowledge if self-cognizance has not been obtained.

People live dreaming, they work dreaming, yet nevertheless they mistakenly believe that they are awakened.

During the normal sleep of the physical body, the ego is enwrapped in the body of desires[20] and wanders in the molecular region[21] like a somnambulist, dreaming, and when it returns into the physical body, when it returns to the "vigil" state, its dreams continue within the individual.

The one who awakens his consciousness no longer dreams; one lives awakened in the internal worlds while the physical body is asleep.

As people awaken their consciousness, accordingly the solar system of Ors will become more and more radiant.

---

20 What people mistakenly call "astral body" is actually the kama rupa, literally "body of desires," an aggregation of our psychological defects.

21 The world of dreams, part of the fifth dimension.

The solar system of Ors is Adam Kadmon,[22] the celestial human born from the water and the fire in the ninth sphere (sex).

The solar system of Ors, the Kosmic Human, needs to be totally awakened in the cell and in the human being, in order to become more and more radiant.

22 An Hebrew term with many applications, including the first manifestation of the abstract space; the archetypal man; humanity; the heavenly man, not fallen into sin.

Chapter 4

Atomic Science

Deep down, the solar system Ors in which we live, move, and have our Being is like a great molecule that develops and unfolds within the spiral organism of the vibrant Milky Way.

The different scientific concepts about atoms are in their depth exclusively provisional [temporary]. Splitting the atom by no means signifies absolute knowledge of the structure of the atom, or about the complex intimate mechanisms of molecules, sub-atomic corpuscles, and electrons. The Saturnian concept of atomic structure is very empirical; any scientific or supra-scientific opinion is very relative and unstable.

We Gnostics emphatically affirm that besides protons, electrons, neutrons, etc., there are many other corpuscles that are still unknown to official science. There is a formidable structure—absolutely unknown to the official science—within the atomic nucleus. The scientists already split the atom in order to release nuclear energy, yet indeed they know nothing about the intimate, intra-corpuscular structure of the electron.

Under the light of the new culture initiated in the world by the Gnostic movement, we can consider the electron like the prime crystallization of what the Hindustanis call Akasha, which is the prime matter of the Great Work, the unique substance from which—by means of chained crystallizations—the multiple substances, the different elements of Nature come to be.

Undoubtedly, the electron is an extraordinary, prime crystallization of a supra-atomic character. Any atom, any electron, has its origin within the living womb of pure Akasha, the primordial substance, the Mulaprakiti of Hindustanis, the Chaos, the universal seminal waters of Genesis, the eternal feminine, symbolized by all the feminine deities of ancient religions, the Great Mother, Isis, Adonia, Insobertha, Rhea, Cybele, Vesta, Mary, Tonantzin, etc.

Undoubtedly, this fundamental substance, this Akasha, this prime matter of the Great Work, is the Divine Mother, Isis, the adorable Virgin of all the ancient religions, always full of grace.

The Father, the First Logos, endowed her with all the grace of his wisdom. The Son, the Second Logos, endowed her with all the grace of his love. The Holy Spirit, the Third Logos, endowed her with all of the grace of his igneous power.

Indeed, in the universe, there is only one basic substance, which when crystallized receives the name matter, and when it does not crystallize, when it remains in its fundamental state, receives the name Universal Spirit of Life.

She initiates her processes of condensation or crystallization when the Third Logos fecundates her with the flaming fire, by means of the sexual connubium of the Word.

She remains in her [virginal] insipid, unsubstantial, odorless state during the cosmic night, during the great pralaya,[23] when the universe that existed ceases to exists. However, the Cosmic Christ, the Second Logos, enters her womb, the great womb, through the fire of the Third Logos that makes her fecund; thus, this is how the Cosmic Christ is born from her and within her in order to be crucified in the worlds. This is why she is always represented with a child in her arms, namely, Isis with the child Horus in her arms, Mary with the God Child in her arms, etc.

Thus, many fields of force are originated under the impulse of the Third Logos within the fecund womb of the Great Mother, where the waves—that we can call pre-matter—are condensed into corpuscles.

Modern scientists know nothing about the mystery of the atomic nucleus, which they consider to be formed by protons and neutrons; they know nothing precise about the nuclear forces.

All planetary material is scientifically constituted by wonderful atoms, which beyond any doubt are considered the smallest particles of the elements.

Every atom is a true universe in miniature. Every atom is a trio of matter, energy, and consciousness. The atom is constituted by a nucleus or a very radiant sun that is charged

23 Sanskrit, a time of repose.

positively with electricity. The infinitesimal electrons, charged negatively, happily spin, dancing around the nucleus. The atomic nucleus is similar in all elements, as well as the electron; the elements vary from each other solely by the number of electrons submitted to the nucleus, and by variations corresponding to their charge.

The atom is a whole solar system in miniature. Exactly what the Sun is to the solar system, and the fecundated egg to the human body, is the atomic nucleus with respect to the whole atomic universe.

It has been said unto us that the diameter of the atomic nucleus can be about one ten thousandth of the whole atom. Thus, like Jupiter to the Sun, it is stated to us that its electrons can measure a tenth of diameter of its nucleus; therefore, in their own scale the electrons circulate in an immensity, a gigantic and deep space like the one that includes in its totality the planet Earth and the other planets of the solar system of Ors.

Nature has many elements, and these are now [as of this writing in 1967] cataloged thanks to the number of electrons from 1 to 96. Hydrogen with one electron has the atomic number 1; helium with two electrons, 2; etc.; thus basically, with two exceptions only, the elements developed within the womb of the Great Mother are different crystallizations from the primordial substance.

There are seven fundamental categories of density amongst the varied elements in Nature.

Each element is sexually attracted by the element that possesses the complementary number of electrons; behold the wonderful manner in which sodium, with an extra electron, is sexually inclined to chlorine, which lacks one electron; their combination forms salt. Here we have sex... Here we have the male and the female of the elements of Nature sexually united.

A positive metal is irresistibly impelled to be sexually combined with a negative metalloid, in an exact proportion to its contrast. This is an extraordinary platonic parallelism of twin

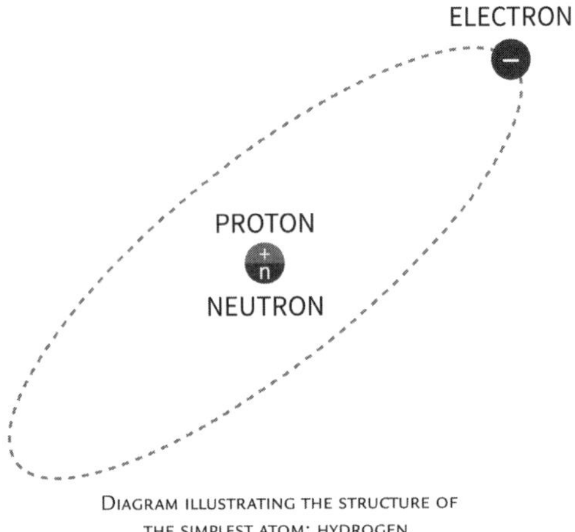

DIAGRAM ILLUSTRATING THE STRUCTURE OF THE SIMPLEST ATOM: HYDROGEN.

souls, which look for their complementary half from which they were separated during the primary creation.

Undoubtedly, the active element in the Sun Christ is an infinite quantity of hydrogen.[24] A hydrogen atom possesses one single electron that spins around its basic nucleus. A hydrogen atom is found at the border between matter in a molecular state and matter in an electronic state. The next state of subtleness of the hydrogen corresponds to free electrons, light, magnetic waves, a spiritual state.

In order to create an helium atom and two sun rays, it is necessary to consume four hydrogen atoms through the sexual energy of the Third Logos that overwhelmingly flows from the center of any atom—and any galaxy and any solar system—uniting opposite poles for new creations. Thus, hydrogen atoms combine with carbon atoms in order to initiate the development of light; namely, masculine atoms of single electron hydrogen bombard the feminine atoms of six electron carbon in order to originate seven electron nitrogen atoms.

24 "Fecundated water, generating water" from Greek hydr-, stem of hydor "water" + French -gène "producing," from gen: generate, genes, genesis, genetic, etc. Hydrogen is the simplest element on the periodic table and is the building block of all forms of matter. Hydrogen is a packet of solar light, the reflection of the cosmic solar intelligence, the Cosmic Christ, which creates and sustains every world. The water is the source of all life. Everything that we eat, breathe and all of the impressions that we receive are in the form of various structures of hydrogen.

Then, nitrogen atoms sexually unite with new hydrogen atoms to become atoms of light-oxygen. When a light-oxygen atom is found in plenitude, one free electron and a certain amount of radiating energy escapes from it; thereafter, an atom of heavy nitrogen is the outcome, that again is sexually bombarded by hydrogen; nevertheless, this time the obtained outcome differs, since another hydrogen atom captures one of the electrons of the nitrogen in order to form one helium atom with two electrons, whereas the nitrogen atom with seven electrons is reduced to a carbon atom with six electrons with which the cycle started, because the end is always equal to the beginning plus the experience of the cycle. That is the law. Thus, this is how the sexual cycle of carbon is closed. Solar light is sexually gestated in the ninth sphere (sex). The great solar light is the chemical and mathematical outcome of the different atomic, sexual processes of carbon.

Hydrogen atoms constitute a bridge between the universal spirit of life and matter of different densities.

The splitting of the atom, the nuclear blasts, release submerged abysmal matter—new, terribly malignant atomic elements: Neptunium (93), Plutonium (94), Americium (95), and Curium (96). Through atomic blasts these infernal types of terribly malignant atomic substances escape from the abyss, and attract to the surface of the Earth and into the mentality of people certain frightfully monstrous psychological characteristics.

The disintegration of the atom is a blasphemy, a scientific madness, that not only brings physical damage to this afflicted world, but also mental, psychic monstrosities, frightful infernal types of abominations, etc.

If instead human beings would study solar energy and learn how to use it intelligently, liquid fuel would be eliminated and the conquest of space would become a fact, on the condition of upright behavior. Where a solar ray of light can reach, human beings too will reach. Solar energy is a million times more powerful than atomic energy. This great molecule, this solar system of Ors, works marvelously thanks to the terrific potential of solar energy.

Earth

Chapter 5

The Ninth Sphere

The Earth is a wonderful organism filled with an intense cosmic vitality. Formidable rocks (inhabited by joyful gnomes[25]), earth, and sand are on the surface of the Earth. The interior of the planetary organism is unknown to official science; indeed, scientists know very little about the interior of our world. It is stated that the temperature of its interior increases progressively in accordance with the increasing depth, in proportion to 12°C.

The earthquake-produced waves in the interior of the planetary organism behave as if they were entering a liquid element, but when the spreading waves approach the surface, they behave as if they were crossing a solid.

The surface layer of the Earth seems to be a crust fifty to sixty kilometers deep. Upon this wonderful crust are found minerals, grounds, sand, and water. Beneath this formidable crust—upon which the entire history of humanity has developed—there is another layer, 3,500 meters thick, composed of magnesium, oxygen, and silicon combined as another form of solid rock.

So far, the scientists know nothing about the Earth's nucleus. They only theorize that its density and temperature are very high, and that it measures approximately 6,500 kilometers in diameter.

From the esoteric point of view, the Earth has nine layers, and the symbol of the infinite is found in the ninth. It is necessary to know that the sacred symbol of the infinite is found in the core of the Earth, in its living nucleus, and has the shape of an eight, tipped-over horizontally.

The brain, heart, and sex of the Genie of the Earth are symbolically placed in the Holy Eight, in the symbol of the infinite. The two opposed circles of the Holy Eight represent

---

25 A term from Paracelsus perhaps derived from Greek genomos, "earth-dweller." Gnomes are elemental intelligences related to the dense, fixed aspect of nature (earth). Every part of nature is alive.

the brain and sex. The center of the Holy Eight is the symbolic seat of the heart. Terrible is the fight of brain against sex, sex against brain, and what is even more terrible and most bitter is the fight of heart against heart.

All organized beings that live on the surface of the Earth are structured in accordance with this symbol.

There is a central atom in the center of the Holy Eight, while the twelve spheres of cosmic vibration gravitate around it. A solar humanity must be developed amidst these twelve spheres. The fetus remains nine months within the maternal womb; similarly, nine ages are necessary for a planetary humanity to be born.

The ninth sphere is sex. The fire and the water are found in the ninth sphere, the origin of worlds, beasts, humans, and gods. Every authentic white initiation[26] begins there. The flaming forge of Vulcan is found in the ninth sphere, Mars descends there in order to re-temper his sword and to conquer the heart of Venus, Hermes in order to clean the Augean stables, and Perseus in order to sever the head of Medusa with his flaming sword. Since ancient times, the descent into the ninth sphere was the greatest ordeal of the supreme dignity of the hierophant, Buddha, Hermes, Jesus, Krishna, Dante, Zarathustra, Quetzalcoatl, Mohammed, Moses, etc.

The symbol of the infinite is an esoteric symbol that can only be known through esotericism. Great initiates state that this symbol is elaborated in pure gold, and it is found exactly in center of the Earth, in the Ninth Sphere. Indeed, the utmost splendors and the thickest darkness are within the living Earth.

We must comprehend the three aspects of the interior of the Earth:

---

26 Initiation comes from the Latin words initiare "originate, initiate," from initium "a beginning." Initiations are moments that mark the beginning of a new stage of development, thus in the development of the consciousness there are initiations it must pass through in order to rise. Throughout our history, the real initiations have not been taught publicly. In this new era, for the first time, we can learn about the initiations the consciousness must pass through. Initiations are stages of spiritual development. Initiation is internal, spiritual, not physical.

- First aspect: minerals, water, fire, etc.
- Second aspect: ultraviolet esoteric zone
- Third aspect: tenebrous infrared zone

The subterranean layers of the Earth represent the kingdom of minerals (the Lithosphere) and the kingdom of metals (the Barysphere), that surround a heart of an incredible density and inertia.

Regarding superior dimensions of space, within the planetary organism there are nine superior concentric spheres, like sublime ineffable regions populated by elemental creatures, masters, devas, etc.

Regarding inferior, submerged, infrared dimensions of space, there are infernal worlds of an increasing density, like concentric spheres, which lead according to Dante's own words:

> *...toward the middle, at whose point unites all heavy substance... That point to which, from every part, is dragged all heavy substance.* –Inferno 34

This is the center of the heart of the Earth, where is found the maximum density and gravity, the fundamental seat of Satan,[27] the infernos.

Where the light shines more clearly, darkness is more intense. That is the law of the analogies of the contraries.

In the center of the heart of the Earth are the chair of Satan and the temple of the Genie of the Earth, the symbol of the infinite, and the angels and demons in an eternal battle.

The nucleus of the Earth has three aspects.

- First: physical aspect
- Second: ultraviolet regions
- Third: infrared regions

The Ninth Sphere (sex) in center of the Earth and in humans is the battlefield between the powers of the light and

27 (Hebrew שטן, opposer, or adversary) Although modern Christians have made Satan into a cartoon character, the reality is very different. Satan is the ego, the Devil or "evil" adversary of God that everybody carries within.

the powers of darkness. The secret key that allows us to enter into the ninth sphere is the Arcanum A.Z.F.,[28] the Sahaja Maithuna.[29]

SHIVA LINGA, SYMBOL OF SHIVA

Let us remember that the symbol of Shiva,[30] the Third Logos, is always the black lingam[31] inserted into the yoni.[32] What is important is to not ejaculate ens seminis[33] during the sexual trance, because the entire ens virtutis[34] of the fire is found within the ens seminis. The Arcanum A.Z.F. is the key that allows us to open the ninth door.

28 The practice of sexual transmutation as couple (male-female), a technique known in Tantra and Alchemy. Arcanum refers to a hidden truth or law. A.Z.F. stands for A (agua, water), Z (azufre, sulfur), F (fuego, fire), and is thus: water + fire = consciousness.

29 Sanskrit: सहज sahaja, "original, natural." मैथुन maithuna, "marriage, sacramental intercourse, a pair or one of each sex." A reference to superior sexuality in which the orgasm is abandoned and lust is replaced by love.

30 Hindu deity, the third aspect of the Trimurti (Brahma, Vishnu, Shiva). The Third Logos. The Holy Spirit. The sexual force. The sephirah Binah.

31 Sanskrit लिङ्ग male sexual organ, also "sign, mark, proof evidence."

32 Sanskrit योनी, female sexual organ.

33 (Latin) Literally, "the entity of semen." A term used by Paracelsus.

34 (Latin) A term used by Paracelsus. Literally, ens is "entity," and virtutis is "strength/power; courage/bravery; worth/manliness/virtue/character/excellence." Virtutis is derived from Latin vir, "man." So, we can translate this as "power entity." Paracelsus stated that the ens virtutis must be extracted from the ens seminis, thus saying that all virtue and excellence is developed from the force within the sexual waters.

Chapter 6

The Sexual Energy

Sex has an 84 year cycle and is governed by the planet Uranus.[35]

In a cyclical manner, the north and south poles of the planet Uranus alternately point towards the Sun. Those poles are the determining factors of the wonderful 84 year cycle in the human species.

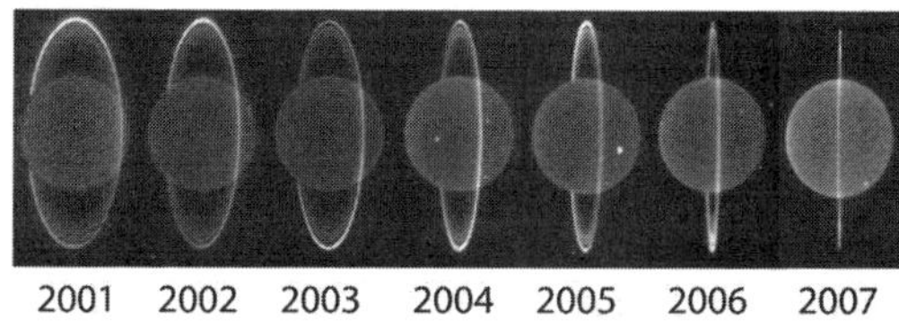

CHANGES OF URANUS PHOTOGRAPHED BY NASA.

If the masculine, positive pole of Uranus is pointed towards the Sun, then the masculine sexual impulse predominates on the Earth; yet, if the feminine, negative pole of Uranus is pointed towards the Sun, then the feminine sexual impulse predominates on the Earth.

For 42 years the masculine sex predominates. For 42 years the feminine sex reigns sovereign.

The history of piracy, the age of Isabel, where masculinity is displayed, like chivalrous adventures, clearly represent the masculine sexual cycle.

This year 1965, in which women reveal their bodies more, and who predominate, command, and protest, clearly indicates the sexual feminine cycle.

---

35 Οὐρανός has etymological roots in Sanskrit वर्‌ष varsá 'rain, cloud, shower', Hittite varša- 'fog, mist', Indo-European*vérs- 'to rain, moisten', Greek eérsē 'dew'. This reveals the role of Uranus / Ouranos influencing our sacred waters, the sexual power, and shines light on many symbols, such as the symbol of dew in the Bible.

In fact, the mature man or woman lives in the opposite sexual atmosphere of the one they were born in. That atmosphere is in fact totally stimulating, and explains with complete exactitude why sexual feelings are often more vigorous and rich in the forties than in the thirties.

HEBE (GREEK)

Sex should be the most elevated creative function. Unfortunately, ignorance reigns sovereign, and humanity is too distant to comprehend the great mysteries of sex.

If we study the book of heaven—the wonderful zodiac—we can then comprehend that the new era of Aquarius[36] is governed by the zodiacal sign of Aquarius, the water carrier.

The symbol of Aquarius is a woman with two full water pitchers, who intelligently attempts to mix the waters of the pitchers. This symbol reminds us of sexual alchemy. In Pisces human beings were mere slaves of their sexual instinct—symbolized by the two fish within the waters of the life—thus in Aquarius human beings must intelligently learn how to combine the waters of existence; they must learn how to transmute their sexual forces.

Aquarius is governed by Uranus, the planet that governs the sexual functions. Thus, it is incongruent and absurd that some isolated individuals and certain pseudo-esoteric schools reject the Maithuna (Sexual Magic)[37] and nonetheless pretentiously boast of being the initiators of the new era.

36 The era of Aquarius began on February 4, 1962.

37 An ancient science known and protected by the purest, most spiritually advanced human beings, whose purpose and goal is the harnessing and perfection of our sexual forces. A more accurate translation of sexual magic would be "sexual priesthood." The word magic is derived from the ancient word magos "one of the members of the learned and priestly class." In ancient times, the priest was always accompanied by a priestess, to represent the divine forces at the base of all creation: the masculine and feminine, the Yab-Yum, Ying-Yang, Father-Mother: the Elohim.

Uranus is one hundred percent sexual, thus in the new era governed by this planet, the human being must know the mysteries of sex in depth. So, to reject the Maithuna (Sexual Magic) signifies in fact to pronounce oneself against the sign of Aquarius, governed by Uranus, the king of sex.

We must remember that the most subtle, most powerful, most refined energy that is produced and marvelously conduced through the human organism is the sexual energy.

By very deeply analyzing the astounding power of the sexual energy, we arrive at the conclusion that it is extraordinarily volatile and very difficult to store and control.

The sexual energy is like a deposit of dynamite; its presence signifies a formidable source of tremendous potentiality, and also a constant danger of a catastrophic explosion.

The sexual energy has its own channels of circulation, its own organized electrical system.

When the sexual energy infiltrates the mechanism of other functions, it can produce great explosions, tremendous biological, physiological, and psychic catastrophes.

The violent and destructive types of manifestations of the sexual energy are generally derived from certain negative psychological attitudes towards sex. Sexual suspicion, fear of sex, sexual prejudices, the cynical, brutal, or obscene sense of sex, etc., obstruct the channels whereby the sexual energy circulates, and therefore the sexual energy deviates and infiltrates other channels, systems, and functions where it produces frightening catastrophes.

The aspect of such catastrophes is usually multifaceted. Sometimes it has the aspect of a fire that flames with passionate wrath, at other times the bitterness of an injurious retort, hurtful words, violent denunciations, etc; all of this and thousands of disgusting subject-matters of the human species are the outcome of the infiltration of the sexual energy into other channels and functions.

People who squander their sexual energy in morbid sexual conversations, who watch pornographic movies, or who read dishonest novels become impotent.

People who miserably spend their time reasoning about the sexual act without fulfilling their sexual functions become impotent; indeed, when—aside from any reasoning— they are going to perform the sexual act, they cannot, and fail.

When imagination and reasoning are poorly used, they can lead us to a psycho-sexual type of impotence. Morbid imagination, the wrong use of imagination, exhausts the sexual energy, and the individual about perform the sexual act fails, becoming impotent.

Excessive reasoning about sex leads to impotence. The one who lives only analyzing the sexual act without performing it, when he is truly ready to actually perform it, must pass through the tremendous surprise that he cannot: he is impotent.

Let our readers not be frightened when arriving at this part of the chapter; it is urgent to study the mysteries of sex, yet to abuse reasoning about sex while excluding the sexual act for an indefinite length of time produces psycho-sexual impotence.

Sub-imagination and infra-imagination exist. Some people—if they wish—can contemplate a person of the opposite sex with purity, nevertheless their sub-imagination and infra-imagination can betray them in the submerged levels of their mind, and thus lead them to perform the coitus in other states of consciousness, whose outcome is usually nocturnal pollutions with abundant loss of seminal liquor.

At this patriarchal headquarters of the gnostic movement in Mexico City constantly arrive many letters from people who complain about having erotic dreams accompanied by nocturnal pollutions.[38] We always answer by advising to those people the Maithuna, Sexual Magic, A.Z.F. (sexual union without loss of semen)[39] as the unique remedy against nocturnal pollutions.

It is clear that by means of daily Maithuna the human being becomes accustomed to refrain in the sexual act in order not to spill the semen. The outcome is that the person

38 "Wet dreams," orgasm during sleep.

39 Orgasm, whether in males or females.

becomes so accustomed to this super effort that when in dreams the person performs the sexual act, then already by habit, by instinct, the person refrains in order to avoid the spilling of the seminal liquor, thus sexual pollution[40] does not take place.

Sex and imagination are intimately associated. To arrive at absolute chastity[41] is impossible if we did not transform the imagination into a pure mirror without the smallest spot.

It is urgent to transform the mechanical and morbid sub-imagination and the automatic and lustful infra-imagination into the imagination of a newborn child. This type of transformation is only possible with the special aid of the Divine Mother Kundalini, the igneous serpent of our magical powers.

Athena, a Greek symbol of the Divine Mother Kundalini.

It is necessary to know how to pray, to know how to beg the divine serpent, asking for the miracle of transforming our subjective and mechanical imagination into the imagination of a newborn child.

Only She, the Divine Mother, the sacred serpent, can transform the morbid sub-imagination and the bestial infra-imagination into the innocent imagination of a newborn child.

A small boy can contemplate a beautiful naked woman in a pure and perfect manner, without feeling the slightest lust.

40 Fornication. See glossary.

41 True chastity is pure sexuality, or the activity of sex in harmony with our true nature. Properly used, the word chastity refers to sexual fidelity or honor.

Indeed, until we are converted and become as innocent as little children, it is impossible to enter into the kingdom of esotericism.

In the physical world, some people have attained perfect chastity, thus they can give themselves the luxury of contemplating the naked body of a person of the opposite sex without feeling any sort of lust. It is clear that such exceptional people believe that they have also achieved absolute chastity in the subconscious territories of the mind, without even remotely suspecting that their sub-imagination and their subjective and mechanical infra-imagination betray them below the surface of their intellectual sphere. These types of exceptional people may have a chaste imagination, but they ignore that their sub-imagination and infra-imagination fornicate frightfully in regions unknown to their reasoning and intellect. When these types of people are submitted to tests of chastity in the superior worlds or within the submerged worlds of nature, when they are placed in situational states and different times of an infraconscious or subconscious type, they fail lamentably.

Many people write to us requesting a remedy for nocturnal pollutions. We always answer these sick people, we always prescribe them Sexual Magic, the Maithuna.

Whosoever becomes accustomed to restrain the sexual act in order not to ejaculate the seminal liquor becomes cured of nocturnal pollutions.

Morbid, lustful dreams are the outcome of the mechanical sub-imagination and the erotic and automatic type of infra-imagination.

If we turn on a television, then before the eyes of the viewer many scenes, pictures, and figures follow one after the other in an automatic manner. Imagination is like a television: any sexual shock turns it on, not only in the intellectual sphere, but also in other submerged territories of the mind.

Any dreamer in the internal worlds can be affected by morbid types of representations. Those representations produce erotic dreams and nocturnal pollutions.

If the dreamer is accustomed to restrain the sexual act, in this case the erotic dream will continue to exist, but without nocturnal pollutions.

If the dreamer has transformed their sub-imagination and infra-imagination into the imagination of an innocent child, then erotic dreams are impossible; they disappear in a radical, total, and definitive manner.

If any esotericist student were submitted to frightening sexual tests in the internal worlds without first having passed through very long periods of daily Sexual Magic, it is clear that the student would fail lamentably, thus losing the seminal liquor through nocturnal pollutions.

Without Sexual Magic, without Maithuna, A.Z.F., it is impossible to move forward on the path of initiation.

When the sexual energy is centrifugal—when it flows from inside towards outside—the outcome is seminal discharges, nocturnal pollutions. Yet, with Maithuna, Arcanum A.Z.F., Sexual Magic, the different currents of sexual energy reverse their course, they become centripetal; then they flow from outside toward the inside. Seminal discharges, nocturnal pollutions, are totally impossible when the sexual energy flows from the exterior towards the interior.

In a molecular, superior level, the sexual energy contains within itself the universal seal or cosmic design of the true human; by means of Sexual Magic we can make this design crystallize in each one of us.

Whosoever wants to achieve in-depth realization must descend into the Ninth Sphere and work with the fire and the water, origin of worlds, beasts, humans, and gods; every authentic white initiation begins there.

There is an intimate relationship between the sexual energy and imagination. The sexual energy is the basic foundation for the realization of our Inner Self.

The initiates who go along the path of the razor's edge are submitted to many sexual tests within the infra-conscious, unconscious, human, sub-human, and infra-human worlds. If initiates do not transform their morbid sub-imagination and mechanical and erotic infra-imagination into the imagination

Jesus Instructs the Samaritan Woman About Sexual Transmutation

"Let marriage be held in honor among all, and let the marriage bed be undefiled; for God will judge the immoral and the adulterous." —Hebrews 13.4

"Be sure of this, that no fornicator or impure man... has any inheritance in the kingdom of Christ and of God." —Ephesians 5.5

of a newborn, innocent child, then it is clear that they will inevitably fail all their sexual tests.

It is necessary to know that in the internal worlds the initiates are placed in other times, places, situations, and different, distinct, diverse, sub-human, infra-human states of consciousness, where they not even remotely remember their studies, the path, etc.

Now our readers will comprehend the urgent necessity of transforming the sub-imagination and the infra-imagination into conscious, objective, and chaste imagination, like the imagination of a newborn child.

Now our readers will comprehend the intimate relationship between sex and imagination.

The sexual energy can transform any person into an angel or into a beast.

In the Western world are many people who mortally hate Sexual Magic; these people justify their absurd hatred with many pretexts. They state that Maithuna, Sexual Magic, "so to say" is only for Eastern people, and that we, the Western people, are not prepared. Those people affirm that with these teachings of sex yoga the only thing that will result is a harvest of black magicians. What is interesting about this is that those types of reactionary, conservative, regressive, and retarded people do not utter a single word against fornication, adultery, prostitution, homosexuality, pederasty, masturbation, etc. All of this seems to them to be quite normal; thus, they do not have any inconvenience in squandering their sexual energy miserably.

The ignorant fornicators from reactionary pseudo-occultism absolutely ignore the secret doctrine of the Savior of the World, the Christian esotericism.

The pseudo-esoteric and pseudo-occultist reaction ignores that the primeval Christian Gnostic sects practiced Maithuna,

Sexual Magic.[42] Maithuna was always taught in all ancient schools of Western mysteries. Maithuna was known among the mysteries of the Templars, among the mysteries of the Aztecs, Mayan, Incas, Chibchas, Zapotecs, Araucans, Toltecs, mysteries of Eleusis, mysteries of Rome, Mithra, Carthage, Tyre, Celtic mysteries, Phoenicians, Egyptian, Druids, and in all the primeval Christian sects, such as the sect of the Essenians, who had their monastery at the shores of the Dead Sea, and one of their most exalted members was the Divine Rabbi of Galilee.

Maithuna, Sexual Magic, is universal. It is known in the mysteries of the North and the South, the East and the West of the world, nevertheless the reactionary, regressive, fornicating pseudo-occultists violently reject it.

The fundamental stone of the authentic and legitimate schools of mysteries is Maithuna, Arcanum A.Z.F., Sexual Magic.

42 Syneisaktism ('sin-ay-sak-tism', from Greek συνεισάκ "to add or bring together"): the practice of a chaste man and woman living together in a spiritual marriage. The term is most closely associated with early and medieval Christianity. Several related terms are used to label such communities, for example, the virgines subintroductae, the agapetae, and the gynaikes syneisaktoi.

Chapter 7

Attraction of the Opposites

The sexual energy of the Third Logos splendidly harmonizes all the functions of the human organism.

The sexual energy is not only perfect, but moreover, it wills for perfection in all existing things.

The sexual energy produces accordance and concordance among each and every one of the specific functions of the human organism.

The sexual energy works in the wonderful laboratory of the human organism, in order to give it higher potentiality and harmony.

The creative energy of the Third Logos always tries to complete in a perfect way each of the marvelous physiological, psychosomatic, and spiritual functions of the human being.

The creative energy of the Third Logos expands, corrects deficiencies, and performs a complete work.

If we consider a man as half a being and woman as the other half of that Being, we then arrive by logical deduction to the amorous attraction of the opposites.

Thirsty for love, souls always wander in search of their other half, their twin soul, from which they have been separated since the dawn of creation.

On the path of life we always need another being who can fill us, who can supply with complete exactitude that which we lack, not only in the physiological aspect, but also in the psychosomatic and spiritual aspects.

Each of our physical and psychic functions needs a very human supplement; this is a natural necessity in every living being.

The mutual combination of elements of nature, the chemical weddings, the sexual combination of opposed elements in order to achieve a perfect whole, constitutes the living foundation of everything that is, of everything that has been, and of everything that will be.

It is demonstrated that the chemical elements are attracted and amorously combined in accordance with the complementary number of electrons.

Every scientist of chemistry knows by means of observation and experience that once the perfect sheath is settled by a number of electrons, sodium with a leftover electron is sexually united to chlorine, which lacks an electron. What is astounding about this, what is marvelous, is that the sodium with an extra electron can never in life be combined with other alkalis that are composed in an analogous manner. In the depths of these wonders, these prodigies of love, we find the marriage of elements and the fundamental stone upon which all chemistry rests.

Without any exaggeration we can affirm that this same principle of sexual attraction of the opposites is always applicable, without any exception, to the attraction and marriage of men and women.

Each organic and psychic function always wants to complement itself, thus the sense of indifference, attraction, or repulsion between man and woman is the exact outcome of an extraordinarily fast, subtle calculation, performed silently.

The sexual sense is more rapid than thought. It makes astonishing calculations. It knows with mathematical precision if a person of the opposite sex before us has all the necessary reciprocal factors to complement us.

Within the human organism, the different glands and their dependent and functional systems act in pairs, some controlling masculine aspects, others controlling the feminine functions. There is a wonderful interchange of chemical substances between the masculine and feminine glands.

The double masculine-feminine aspect of the pituitary gland is astonishing. Any scientist knows very well that the anterior lobe of the pituitary gland is masculine and that the posterior is feminine.

The masculine and feminine glands harmoniously coordinate all the biological functions within the human organism.

Venus and Mars control the pituitary and pineal glands. Whilst in the pituitary gland Venus wants to sleep, in the pineal gland Mars wants to continue fighting.

The same fight between Venus and Mars is repeated in the neck. Venus controls the thyroid and Mars the parathyroid.

The cortex and the medulla of the suprarenal glands always represent masculine and feminine counterparts that lead us to fight or flight.

The union of these sexual masculine-feminine elements in each one of the glands of the human organism is wisely symbolized in the images of Tibetan Tantra,[43] where each god is accompanied by a goddess or feminine Shakti.[44]

Terrible are the tragedies in the world. From fourteen years of age, each man and woman begin searching for their sexual complement. Any particular man can find in some woman his complement for a certain specific function, yet it may be that only with another woman he finds the complement for his fundamental center of gravity. The woman is no exception in this. Now we can better explain to ourselves the tragic, sexual cause of the infamous love triangles that always end in divorce or gunshots. These fatal love triangles cease to exist only with virtue, only by fulfilling the Christian commandment that you shall not commit adultery.

What is ideal in these matters of love is to find the other half, the other half-orange, the twin soul.

Only the total and perfect complement can give us inexhaustible happiness; unfortunately this is too much to ask,

---

43 Sanskrit for "continuum" or "unbroken stream." Tantra refers first (1) to the continuum of vital energy that sustains all existence, and second (2) to the class of knowledge and practices that harnesses that vital energy, thereby transforming the practitioner. "In the view of Tantra, the body's vital energies are the vehicles of the mind. When the vital energies are pure and subtle, one's state of mind will be accordingly affected. By transforming these bodily energies we transform the state of consciousness." –The 14th Dalai Lama

44 (शक्ति Sanskrit, literally "force, power, energy"; also transliterated as Sakti) From the root sakt, which means "to be able, to do." In Hinduism, shakti is symbolized as a goddess, the wife of Shiva, the Third Logos, the sephirah Binah. The feminine aspect of Binah. A personification of primal energy. Symbolized by a yoni, a female sexual organ.

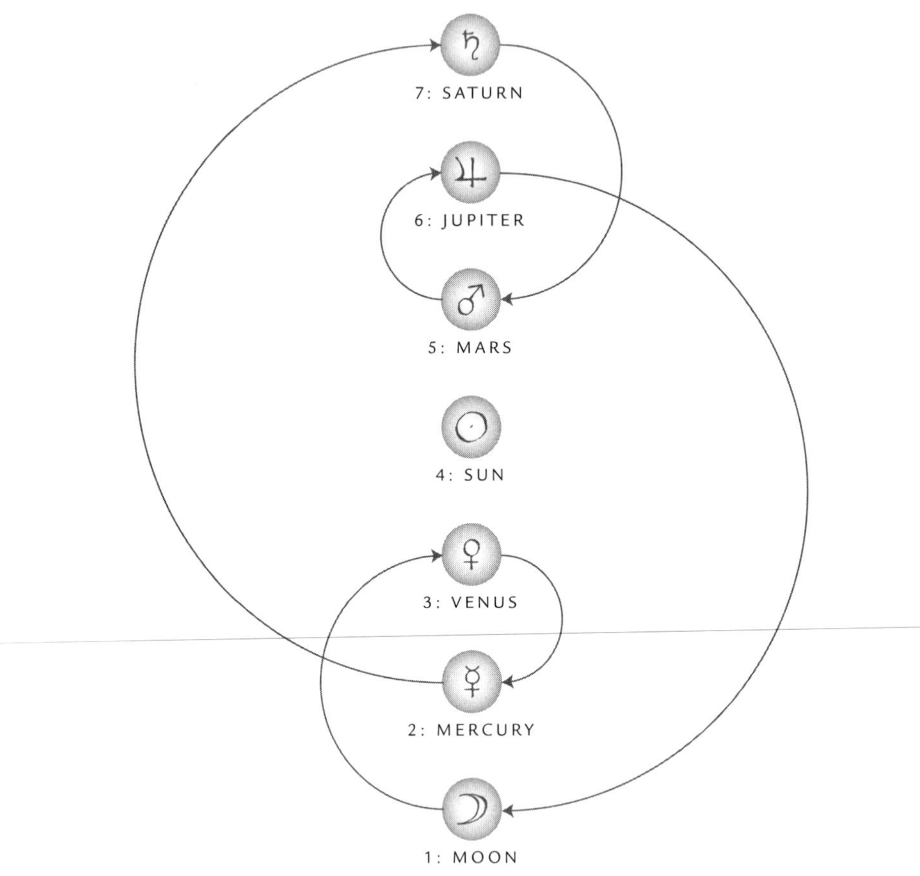

Sexual Complements of the Seven Planets

since we do not deserve that much, given that all of us are full of karmic debts.

In the field of conjugal life, we have been able to verify that sometimes the man leads and other times the woman. In every home there is one who leads and another who is led. Do not confuse this with commanding and to be commanded.

Astrologically speaking, we will say that Venus must lead the Moon, Mercury must lead Venus, Saturn must lead Mercury, Mars must lead Saturn, Jupiter must lead Mars, and the Moon must lead Jupiter. It is clear that for this, it is necessary to know which planet guides our life.[45]

These wise astrological combinations, as we give them here, signify mutual attraction and a perfect sexual complement. Any other sexual unions outside of this order are absurd and even illegitimate, because they violate the sexual nature of those involved, leaving in them deep psychic wounds, very difficult to heal.

The Mercurial man who adores a beautiful Venusian woman because of the love and sweetness that she radiates, can remove her from her romantic laziness and give unto her the Mercurial lightness that she needs.

The Jupiterian woman madly in love with a Martian man can extinguish his violence by conducting his energy in an edifying manner.

The attraction of the opposites has its origin in a divine, ineffable cosmic model.

The Lunar type always tends to move towards the Venusian, the Venusian type moves towards the Mercurial, the Mercurial type moves towards the Saturnian, the Saturnian type moves towards the Martian, the Martian type moves towards the

45 "Every human being can know to what ray he belongs by merely counting the transverse lines on his forehead. Those who have a single line belong to the Lunar Ray. Those who have two lines belong to the Mercurian Ray. Those who have three lines belong to the Venusian Ray. Those who have four lines belong to the Solar Ray. Those who have five lines belong to the Martian Ray. Those who have six lines belong to the Jupiterian Ray. Those who have seven lines belong to the Saturnian Ray." – Samael Aun Weor, *Seven Words*

Jupiterian, and the Jupiterian type turns around and goes towards the Lunar.

Upon this marvelous base of cosmic combinations, the human types can be combined in order to establish perfect marriages upon the face of the Earth.

The Gnostic couples working intensely in the flaming forge of Vulcan, within the Ninth Sphere (sex), can by means of the Maithuna (Sexual Magic) gain what the enemies of sex cannot gain, even if they declare themselves vegetarian and torture themselves during their whole life by living a hermits life.

The great force that can liberate or enslave the human being is in sex.

Chapter 8

The Sexual Hydrogen Si-12

It is urgent to know that there are twelve fundamental basic hydrogens in the universe. The twelve basic hydrogens are arranged in tiers in accordance with the twelve categories of matter.

The twelve categories of matter exist in all creation; let us remember the twelve salts of the zodiac, the twelve spheres of cosmic vibration within which a solar humanity must be developed.

All the secondary hydrogens, whose varied densities go from 6 to 12283, are derived from the twelve basic hydrogens.

In Gnosticism, the term hydrogen has a very extensive significance. Indeed, any simple element is hydrogen of a certain density. Hydrogen 384 is found in water, 192 in the air, while 96 is wisely deposited in the animal magnetism, emanations of the human body, X-rays, hormones, vitamins, etc.

By now, the brothers and sisters of the Gnostic movement are very acquainted with hydrogens 48, 24, 12, and 6, given that we have studied them in our previous Christmas messages. Hydrogen 48 corresponds to chlorine (CI), atomic weight 35.5. Hydrogen 24 corresponds to fluorine (F), atomic weight 19. Hydrogen 12 corresponds to hydrogen of chemistry (H), atomic weight 1.

Carbon, nitrogen, and oxygen have the atomic weights of 12, 14, and 16. Hydrogen 96 corresponds to bromine (Br), atomic weight 80. Hydrogen 192 corresponds to iodine, atomic weight 127.

This most interesting subject-matter about hydrogens belongs to the branch of esoteric chemistry or Gnostic chemistry, and since it is quite difficult, for the good of our students we prefer to study it little by little in each one of our Christmas messages.

Let us now study the famous sexual hydrogen Si-12, the marvelous creative hydrogen that is wisely elaborated in the factory of the human organism.

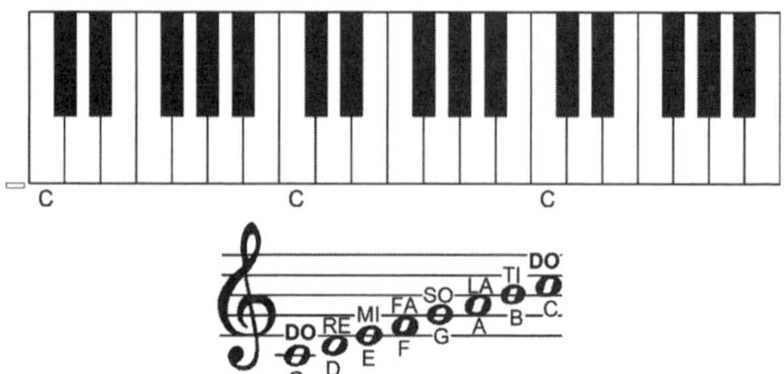

MUSICAL OCTAVES ON PIANO KEYBOARD (TOP) AND MUSICAL NOTATION (BOTTOM)

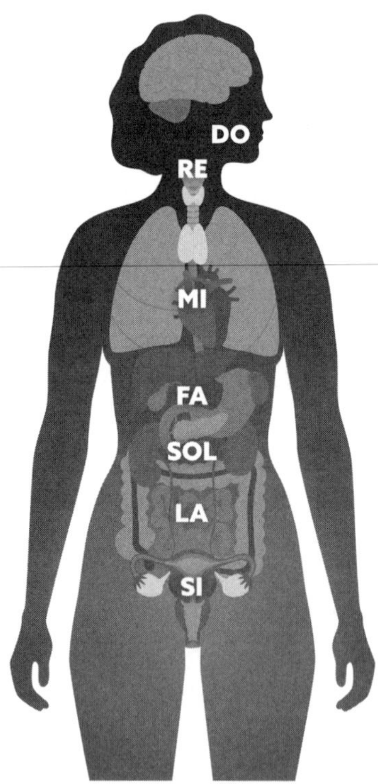

THE OCTAVE OF HUMAN DIGESTION

Within the human organism, the passive food on the plate passes through many transformations, refinements and subtle changes, that are processed within the musical scale DO, RE, MI, FA, SOL, LA, SI.

The transformation of the passive food of the plate begins with the note DO, the resulting chyme of the first stage of transformation follows with note RE, the very refined food that osmotically passes into the sanguineous fluid continues with the note MI, and so on, successively, other processes follow, until the best element of the entire organism becomes elaborated: that is, the wonderful elixir, the seminal liquor, with its hydrogen 12 in the note SI.

The sexual hydrogen Si-12 is found in the semen;[46] that hydrogen is the creative power of the Third Logos.

The first musical octave, DO-RE-MI-FA-SOL-LA-SI, corresponds exactly to the manufacture of the sexual hydrogen Si-12 within the human organism.

A very special shock[47] by means of Maithuna (Sexual Magic) allows the sexual hydrogen SI-12 to pass to a second musical octave, DO-RE-MI-FA-SOL-LA-SI, whose outcome becomes the crystallization of the sexual hydrogen Si-12 into the extraordinary form of the astral body. This is what is called "to transmute lead into gold." It is urgent to transmute the flesh and the blood in the astral body.

A second shock[48] by means of Maithuna (Sexual Magic) allows the sexual hydrogen Si-12 to pass to a third musical octave DO-RE-MI-FA-SOL-LA-SI, whose outcome becomes the crystallization of the sexual hydrogen Si-12 in the extraordinary form of the mental body (paradisiacal body).

---

46 Latin, literally "seed of plants, animals, or people; race, inborn characteristic; posterity, progeny, offspring," figuratively "origin, essence, principle, cause." In other words, semen is not just a fluid in masculine bodies. Semen refers to the sexual energy of any creature or entity. In Gnosis, "semen" is a term used for the sexual power of both masculine and feminine bodies.

47 Through the third initiation of Major Mysteries. Read *The Perfect Matrimony* by Samael Aun Weor.

48 Through the fourth initiation of Major Mysteries.

A third shock[49] by means of Maithuna (Sexual Magic) allows the hydrogen Si-12 to pass to a fourth musical octave DO-RE-MI-FA-SOL-LA-SI, whose outcome is the crystallization of the sexual hydrogen Si-12 in the magnificent form of the body of the conscious will or causal body.

The sexual hydrogen Si-12 is seed or fruit, and what is astounding is that it always crystallizes in organisms of flesh and bone. Let us remember that the physical body is the outcome of the sexual hydrogen Si-12. The astral body also becomes the outcome of it, but through the special act Maithuna (union of the phallus and the uterus without spilling the semen). Thus the astral body is also a body of flesh and bone, a flesh that does not come from Adam,[50] but a flesh-product of the sexual hydrogen Si-12.

The true mental body is also the product of Maithuna (Sexual Magic) and of the sexual hydrogen Si-12. This is a paradisiacal body, a body of perfection, a body of flesh and bone, but flesh that does not come from Adam.

The body of conscious will, also called causal body, is also the outcome of the sexual act Maithuna without spilling the semen. The body of conscious will or causal body is the outcome of the crystallization of the sexual hydrogen Si-12.

The authentic astral body, the true mental body, and the legitimate causal body constitute the solar bodies, the existential superior bodies of the Being.

Whosoever builds in the Ninth Sphere the superior existential bodies of the Being, the solar bodies, can and has all the right to incarnate their real Being, their immortal triune spirit, Atman-Buddhi-Manas[51]—or Divine Spirit, Spirit of Life, and Human Spirit (Innermost, Spiritual Soul, and Human Soul).

---

49 Through the fifth initiation of Major Mysteries.

50 In Western religions, the first human being and first fornicator. The solar astral body is not made by fornication, (orgasm), so is not a product of the sinning Adam.

51 "Atman: the Being, the divine immortal spark, has two souls that in esotericism are called Buddhi and Manas." —Samael Aun Weor, *Tarot and Kabbalah*

Then, when arriving at these initiatic heights, it is stated that a new human being has been born, the Son of Man, a new master of the day, a master of the mahamanvantara.[52]

The physical body is sustained with the hydrogen 48, the surplus of this hydrogen becomes hydrogen 24, with which the astral body is fed. The surplus of hydrogen 24 becomes hydrogen 12 (do not confuse with the sexual hydrogen Si-12). The hydrogen 12 feeds the mental body. The surplus of hydrogen 12 becomes hydrogen 6, with which the body of conscious will or authentic causal body is fed.

The creation of the solar bodies is a subject-matter related to Maithuna, Sexual Magic, without spilling the semen, and it is performed in the flaming forge of Vulcan,[53] in the Ninth Sphere (sex).

This is a work bitterer than bile; daily sexual connection of the same man with the same woman, over twenty or thirty years, without ever spilling even a single drop of semen, without allowing the semen to leave our organism.

The Twice-born, the one who is born within the superior worlds as a master of the mahamanvantara, the one who leaves the Ninth Sphere for the fact of having completed its work, never ever can return to the Ninth Sphere again, because this would be a crime, similar to the child who, after been born, wanted to enter again within the womb of his mother.

Any Twice-born is a child of the Mother Kundalini, and if he wants to progress he must love his Divine Mother; he must never forget his Mother.

To the Twice-born, the sexual act remains forbidden for all eternity, thus he must attain absolute chastity in all the territories of the mind.

---

52 Sanskrit, great period of cosmic activity.

53 The Latin or Roman name for the Greek god Ἥφαιστος Hephaestus, known by the Egyptians as Ptah. A god of fire with a deep and ancient mythology, commonly remembered as the blacksmith who forges weapons for gods and heroes. Vulcan is very important in the tradition of Alchemy. In Hinduism, he is symbolized by Tvastri, later called Visvakarma.

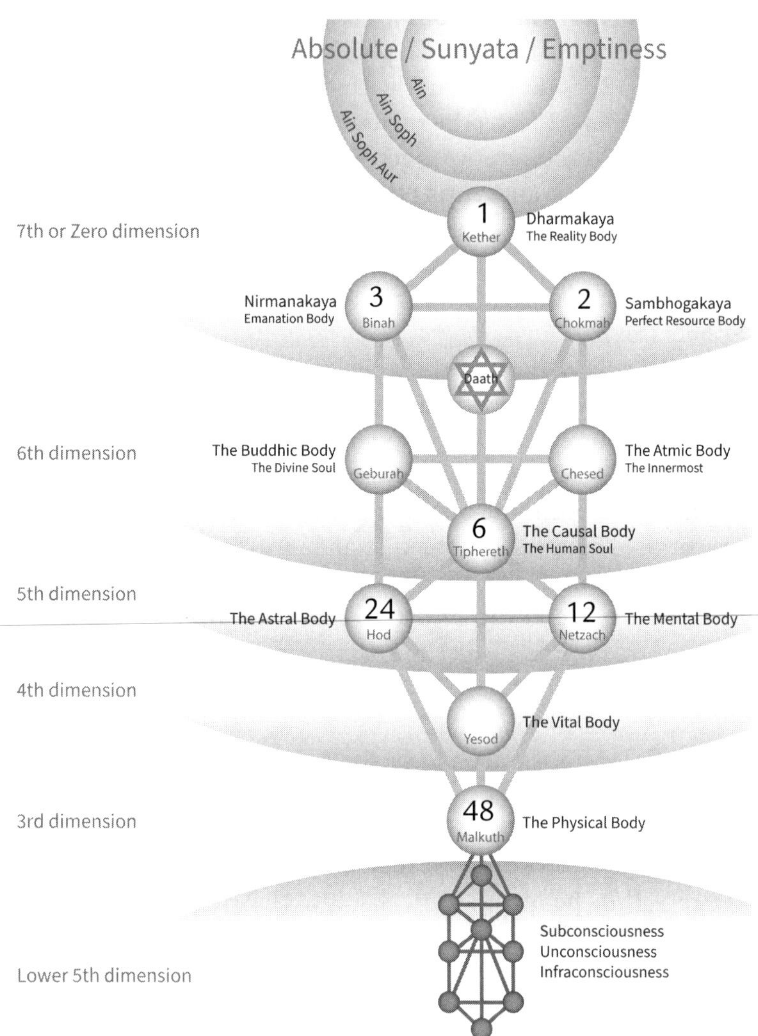

Hydrogens and the Bodies of the Being on the Tree of Life (Kabbalah)

Chapter 9

The Lunar Bodies

All the very esoteric and very occult schools base their studies on the following Theosophical septenary:

THEOSOPHICAL SEPTENARY

1. Atman (the innermost)
2. Buddhi (the spiritual soul)
3. Superior manas (the human soul)
4. Inferior manas (mental body)
5. Kama rupa (body of desires or astral)
6. Linga sarira (vital body)
7. Sthula sarira (physical body)

Atman is the lord, the Innermost. Buddhi is the spiritual soul. Superior manas is the human soul.

The Innermost, the lord, has two souls. The first is the spiritual soul (buddhi). The second is the human soul (superior manas, causal principle).

The two souls must work under the direction of the lord, yet this is only possible in masters. While the human soul works, the spiritual soul plays.

The spiritual soul is feminine, and the human soul is masculine. In the masters, the spiritual soul is usually pregnant with fruits that, when they are born, must be elaborated by the human soul.

People feel very proud with their mental body, because with it we reason, discuss, project, etc., however this mental body is one hundred percent lunar; all animals have it in a residual state.

People live in the world of animal passions and enjoy their passional desires, because the emotional vehicle that we possess is only an animal lunar body with beastly desires.

The vital body is the tetradimensional body, the Linga Sarira of Hindustanis, the living foundation of all the physical, chemical, caloric, perceptive activities, etc. Indeed, the vital body is only the superior section of the physical body, the tetradimensional part of the physical body.

Many clairvoyants usually see a sweet creature of a blue electrical color, very beautiful, within the mental and desire vehicles that is easily confused with the human soul or body of the conscious will (causal body).

In fact, the intellectual animal still does not have a causal body. The beautiful blue creature that clairvoyants see within the lunar vehicles is what in Zen Buddhism is called Buddhadhatu,[54] the essence,[55] a fraction of the sacred human soul within us.

No intellectual animal has a causal body. No intellectual animal has incarnated the immortal triad. If someone were to incarnate his divine immortal triad, he would immediately stop being an intellectual animal and become a human being.

Only by fabricating the solar bodies can we give ourselves the luxury of incarnating the divine immortal triad Atman-Buddhi-Manas.

If we want to ascend, we must first descend. We can fabricate the solar bodies only by descending into the Ninth Sphere, in order to incarnate the immortal triad and become human beings.

At the present time, we are only intellectual animals. The unique thing that adorns us is the intellect, thus if the intellect were to be taken from us, we would become very useless animals, worse than orangutans and gorillas, stupid, defenseless, beastly creatures.

Zen Buddhism considers the lunar bodies as mental forms that we must dissolve, reduce to dust.

The lunar bodies are common property of all beasts, including the intellectual beast mistakenly called a human being.

We can give ourselves the luxury of incarnating the immortal triad in order to become true human beings only by fabricating the solar bodies.

---

54 (Sanskrit), which means "essence of the Buddha," (from धातु dhatu, "element, primary element, cause, mineral").

55 Chinese 體 ti, "substance." See glossary.

The solar bodies are the outcome of a conscious work done on oneself.

Only by descending into the Ninth Sphere can we fabricate the solar bodies and incarnate the immortal triad, in order to be born in the superior worlds as new masters of the mahamanvantara.

During the dream hours and after death, the intellectual animal lives with lunar bodies within the supersensible worlds. These bodies are cold and ghostly.

The solar bodies are radiating, sublime, living flames. Remember that angels, archangels, masters, etc., use solar bodies.

The authentic astral solar body is a vehicle of flesh and bone, but flesh that does not come from Adam, a body of incalculable beauty and supreme happiness.

The legitimate mental solar body is a paradisiacal body, a body of flesh and bone, but flesh that does not come from Adam, a body of a feminine, receptive nature.

The true mental solar body is beyond reasoning; it is a vehicle of comprehension. Those who possess the true mental body do not need to accept or to reject, they comprehend, and that is all.

The authentic mental solar body has three hundred thousand clans or magnetic centers, and each clan must vibrate to the same tone without any effort. The mental solar body with its three hundred thousand clans is formidable, wonderful.

The adept who possess a totally developed mental solar vehicle, receives and comprehends the truth from moment to moment, without the tremendous battle of thought.

The legitimate body of conscious will allows the adept to have conscious immortality.

The legitimate body of conscious will allows the adept to perform actions born from conscious will; it allows the adept to determine circumstances.

Any master who has been born within the superior worlds must eliminate the lunar bodies; these substitute our animal remnants that come from ancient times.

Common and ordinary disincarnated souls dressed with their lunar bodies[56] seem cold, ghostly, unconscious somnambulists, living in the past.

The intellectual animal is one hundred percent lunar, and indeed, is not a true human being.

Only by fabricating the solar bodies do we become true human beings.

56 In a later lecture, Samael Aun Weor explained that he used the phrase "lunar bodies" in a similar way to how we call each other "human beings," even though we are not. That is, we are being polite, but the truth is something else. He said: "Only a human has [internal] bodies; the 'intellectual animal' has no bodies. That he has a 'lunar astral body' is not so. The only thing that the 'intellectual animal' has inside are demons. It's a lot of devils, but it doesn't have more... They are the 'I's,' which penetrate and interpenetrate each other... What I said in one of my books about lunar bodies, I was referring to the egos and the three main demons that everyone carries inside, which are the demon of desire, the demon of the mind and the demon of evil will, which they act as astral, mental and causal, but they are nothing but demons. So, practically, the 'intellectual animal' does not have any kind of bodies: neither solar, nor lunar, nor anything; It's a bunch of devils that you have to turn to dust, so that the consciousness remains free and can see, hear, touch or palpate the great realities of the universe..." —How to Develop Ourselves into a Complete Human Being and Eliminate Our Defects

Chapter 10

The Pluralized "I"

Writers who affirm the existence of one ego or a permanent and immutable "I" are sincere but mistaken individuals with very good intentions. It is urgent to know that we have a pluralized "I" within our lunar animal bodies. Each sensation, each emotion, each thought, each feeling, passion, hatred, violence, jealousy, wrath, greed, lust, envy, pride, laziness, gluttony, etc., are constituted by small "I's" that are not bound among themselves nor have any coordination with each other whatsoever. Thus, there is not a complete, unitotal "I," but a multitude of grudging, quarrelsome, and noisy "I's" that fight with each other, that struggle among themselves for supremacy.

The monks of Mount Athos monastery like to become cognizant of all these small "I's" and to learn how to handle them, how to pass them from one center to another, etc. The monks kneel down, and when lifting their arms with their bent elbows they say, "ego" aloud and prolonging the sound, while simultaneously they try to locate the point of their organism where the word ego ("I") resonates; the purpose of this exercise is to feel the "I," to voluntarily pass it from one center to another.

The "I's" that we have within the lunar bodies are true demons created by ourselves. Any given "I" follows automatically another given "I," and some appear accompanied by others, but in all this there is no order, no true unity, there are only accidental associations, small groups that are associated in an unconscious and subjective manner. Each one of these small "I's" only represents a very small part of the totality of our functions; however, each one always mistakenly believes to be the whole.

When the intellectual animals (mistakenly called human beings) say "I," they have the impression that they speak of themselves in their totality, yet in fact, it is only one of those small "I's" of their legion that speaks through them.

The "I" who today is swearing fidelity before the Gnostic altar believes to be the whole, the only one, the complete person, but it is only one among the many "I's" of the legion. When that "I" falls from its place of command, another "I" who is an enemy of Gnosis occupies its place, then the subject who seemed to be very enthused with Gnosis is turned into an enemy, attacking our movement, our doctrine, etc.

The "I" who today is swearing eternal love to its better half has the impression of being the only one, the boss, the complete person, and says, "I adore you, I love you, I give my life to you, etc.," but when that enamored "I" is displaced from its place of command by another "I," then we see the subject abandoning its better half, and falling in love with someone else, etc.

All these small "I's" are true demons who live within the lunar bodies. All these small "I's" are fabricated within the five cylinders of the human machine. These five cylinders are thought, emotion, movement, instinct, sex. In our previous Christmas messages we already spoke very widely about the five centers of our organic machine.

It is lamentable that because of a lack of wisdom, we "human beings" are fabricating innumerable demons within the five cylinders of our organic machine, who rob part of our consciousness and of our life.

It is also very true and beyond any doubt that sometimes other people's demons or "I's"—created by other people—insert themselves within our lunar bodies. Those "I's" from other people rob part of our consciousness; they lodge within any of the five cylinders of our human machine and for such reason become part of our ego ("I").

Indeed, the intellectual animal does not have true individuality, does not have a permanent center of gravity, nor a true sense of moral responsibility.

The only thing of value, the only important thing that we have within our lunar bodies, is the Buddhata, the sacred Essence, the psychic material that unfortunately is squandered by the different entities which in their conjunction constitute the ego, the pluralized "I."

Many pseudo-occult and pseudo-esoteric schools divide the "I" in two. They emphatically asseverate that we have a divine, immortal, superior "I," and believe that superior "I" or divine ego must totally control and dominate the inferior "I." This concept is totally false, because superior and inferior are two sections of the same thing.

The "I" enjoys being divided between superior and inferior. The "I" enjoys thinking that part of itself is divine, eternal, immortal. The "I" enjoys being praised, worshiped, placed on altars, canonized, etc.

Indeed, that "superior I," that divine ego, does not exist. The only thing that we have within the lunar bodies is the Essence and a legion of "I's," and that is all.

Atman, the Being, has nothing to do with any type of "I." The Being is the Being and is beyond any type of "I." Our real Being is impersonal, cosmic, ineffable, and terribly divine.

Unfortunately, intellectual animals cannot incarnate their real Being (Atman-Buddhi-Manas) because they only have lunar bodies, and the lunar bodies could not withstand the tremendous electrical voltage of our true Being, so we would die.

The demons that live inside the lunar bodies are not imprisoned within those animal bodies; they enter and leave; they travel to different places or subconsciously wander around the different molecular regions of nature.

After death, the pluralized "I" continues within the lunar bodies, projecting itself from within them to any place of nature.

Mediums[57] from spiritism or spiritualism lend their matter or physical vehicles to the "I's" of the dead. Those "I's," even when they give proof of their identity, even if they demonstrate to truly be the invoked dead, are not the real Being of the deceased.

57 "Channelers."

Epilepsy is the karma[58] that mediums suffer in their later lives. Any epileptic person was a medium spiritist or spiritualist in its past life.

Not all the entities that constitute the animal ego ("I") return to this world in order to reincorporate themselves or to be reborn in a new human organism. Some of those entities or small "I's" separate from their group in order to enter into the infernal worlds of nature or submerged mineral kingdom; some other entities enjoy reincorporating themselves within organisms from the inferior animal kingdom, like horses, donkeys, dogs, etc.

The masters of the White Lodge usually help some remarkable souls, deceased, who have sacrificed themselves on behalf of humanity.

When we proposed to investigate Pancho Villa, the great hero of the Mexican revolution, we found him within the infernal worlds still obsessed with the idea of killing; he was menacing all the inhabitants of the underworld with his pistol. Nevertheless, this Pancho Villa from the submerged mineral kingdom is not the whole of him. The best of Pancho Villa lives in the molecular world. Certainly, he did not reach the intermediate liberation that allows some disincarnated souls to enjoy some vacations in the different molecular and electronic kingdoms of nature, therefore he remains at the threshold, waiting for the opportunity in order to enter into a new womb. That which will be reincorporated from the one who was Pancho Villa, will never be the Pancho Villa from the infernal worlds, the terrible assassin, but the best values of the General, those values that sacrificed themselves on behalf of humanity, those values that gave their blood on behalf of the freedom of an oppressed people. The disincarnated General—better said, the truly useful values of the General—will return, will be reincorporated; the great law will pay for his sacrifice by making him the chief magistrate of the nation.

We have mentioned General Pancho Villa as an illustration for our readers, because this man received special aid due to

58 Actions have consequences. Karma is cause and effect, the law of nature that establishes equilibrium.

his great sacrifice on behalf of humanity. Nevertheless, there are people in the world who could never receive this aid, because if everything that they have of animal and criminal was taken from them, nothing would remain. Those types of human beasts must enter into the devolutions of the worlds of nature.

A certain initiate underwent an unspeakable suffering because—despite reaching perfect chastity in the physical world—within the infernal worlds he failed in all the tests of chastity. So, the initiate mortified himself, cried out and begged, requesting for the superior assistance of his own Mother Kundalini. Thus, his Divine Mother helped him. She, the igneous serpent of our magical powers, interceded, begged for him, for her son, for the initiate; thus, he was called to judgment before the courts of karma.

The terrible lords of karma judged him and condemned him to the abyss, to the outer darkness where only weeping and gnashing of teeth are heard.

So, when the initiate, filled with infinite terror, heard the frightful sentence, he saw how the cosmic executioner unsheathed his sword and threateningly raised it and directed it against the frightened brother; then he felt that something moved within his interior, and, astonished, he saw a fornicator "I" exiting his lunar bodies, an entity that he had created on his own in ancient reincarnations. Thus, the perverse fornicator entity entered the devolutions of the infernal worlds. Thereafter, the initiate felt himself free of those internal bestialities that had much tormented him.

Indeed, the ego is a sum of diverse, different entities. There is no permanent and immutable "I." The only thing that exists within our lunar bodies is a pluralized "I" (a legion of devils).

Padmasambhava (male) and Yeshe Tsogyal (female), who established Tantra in Tibet

"Unite male and female energies... female assisting male and male assisting female... ...practice to perfection the skill of retaining your seed-essence [semen, bodhichitta]; be attentive to obstacles and hostile powers [your egos, defects, vices]; if the samaya [chastity] is impaired strive to restore it. About the body: do not let it slip into old habits [of lust and orgasm] or you will become like ordinary men and women [who are animals]... About speech: concentrate upon mantra and energy flows; without energy control your sexual activity is fornication; properly execute the exercises of 'drawing up' [the spine] and 'saturating' [brain and heart] and with the [iron] nails of your imagination apply an hermetic seal [to prevent any loss of energy]. ...If seed-essence [semen, bodhichitta] is lost in actuality [through orgasm] the karma of slaying a Buddha is incurred; at all costs gain self-control [over lust and orgasm]. Absorb yourself intently in [comprehension of] the experience of desire, for without [comprehension] the mysteries have no meaning; desire transmuted into purity bliss [samadhi] is the goal fulfilled. Preserve constant cognition of the primal purity of experience [Voidness, the Absolute]; protect the samaya [of chastity] like your body and life, for if it is broken there is no authority to restore it."

—Yeshe Tsogyal, 8th cent. AD

Chapter 11

Kundalini

When addressing Eastern occultism on the subject of Tantric esotericism, we affirm that there is much material to investigate, to study, to analyze.

Throughout the entire continent of Asia there are multitudes of schools that agree with the virtue of chastity and the non-ejaculation of the seminal fluid; some are partisans of the system of celibacy or brahmacharya,[59] others practice Maithuna or moderate sexual connection and without attachment, but unfortunately with orgasm and the ejaculation of the precious seminal fluid.

The legitimate White Tantric schools of India, China, Tibet, Japan, etc., teach the Sahaja Maithuna (Sexual Magic) without the spilling of the seminal fluid.

In certain very incomplete Tantric schools of India, the Sahaja Maithuna (Sexual Magic) is performed only once in a lifetime, under the direction of a guru, who supervises the awakening of the sacred fire and who with magnetic passes and laying of hands intelligently guides its ascension through the medullar canal. We are informed that before performing this work of sex yoga, both the male and the female sadhaka[60] pass through an intensive preparation in the techniques of Hatha Yoga,[61] mudras,[62] bandhas,[63] kriyas,[64] pratyahara,[65] dha-

59 "...self-restraint, particularly mastery of perfect control over the sexual organ or freedom from lust in thought, word and deed." —Swami Sivananda. Brahmacharya is chastity: sexual purity, meaning that the orgasm is avoided, forbidden. One renounces the low, animal pleasure of the orgasm in order to gain the higher, spiritual bliss of the soul.

60 Sanskrit, spiritual practitioner.

61 Sanskrit, a series of exercises to stretch and loosen the physical body. Originally intended to be a form of exercise to prepare for meditation, the common type of Hatha Yoga does not contain any exercises for the awakening of the consciousness or the elimination of the ego.

62 Sanskrit, "mystic seal." Here, a reference to postures or positions.

63 Sanskrit, "to bind together." Here, postures in Hatha Yoga.

64 Sanskrit, "action, deed, effort," various yoga techniques.

65 Sanskrit, withdrawal from the senses, step five of Raja Yoga.

rana,[66] dhyana,[67] etc. These Tantric yogis consider Hatha and Raja Yoga[68] to be intimately related, forming a total whole. All these practices lead yogi and yogini towards Maithuna (Sexual Magic). In this act, according to the instructions we have received, they apply the Khechari[69] and Vajroli Mudras,[70] and after having initiated the dance of Shiva and Shakti, touching each others backs, sit to meditate–the yogi rests his spine against the yogini's spine–in order to gain complete mental, respiratory, and emotional control. Thereafter, they connect sexually, either in Siddhasana[71] or Vajrasana[72] [postures]. Sometimes, the yogini is lifted into the air by vestals so that the yogi can connect with her in Urdhva padmasana[73] in order to facilitate the Oordhvareta.[74] Then they both absorb the Shakti (sexual energy) of their own semen [sexual forces], which then rises to Shiva in the brain.

All of this information–sourced from Hindustan–states that after attaining the immobility of manas,[75] prana,[76] and apana,[77] the yogi and yogini attain the semenation of their brain, thus definitely raising their Kundalini. This Hindu practice, however, is only for the Yogavatars.

---

66 Sanskrit, one-pointed concentration, step six of Raja Yoga.

67 Sanskrit, meditation, step seven of Raja Yoga.

68 Sanskrit, "Royal Yoga." The science of meditation, especially as described by Patanjali in his *Yoga Sutras.*

69 A practice from the Hindu Kundalini Yoga tradition in which the tongue was previously cut so it could be folded backwards to close the posterior portion of the nostrils. Samael Aun Weor said this practice is not necessary, and is "unfortunate."

70 The vajroli referred to here is another Hindu practice rejected for contemporary use, as it is unnecessary, deprecated, and dangerous.

71 Seated, cross-legged position.

72 Another seated, cross-legged position.

73 A handstand posture, not recommended for contemporary use.

74 or Urdhvareta. Sanskrit; urdhva ,"upwards" + reta, "seed" thus literally meaning to "send the seed upwards." "An Oordhvareta Yogi is one in whom the seminal energy has flown upwards into the brain as Ojas Sakti. There is now no possibility of the semen going downwards [out] by sexual excitement." –Swami Sivananda.

75 Sanskrit; in general use, "mind."

76 Sanskrit, life force, sexual power, and breath.

77 Sanskrit, the vital energy that carries downward unassimilated food and drink. An aspect of prana.

The *Kama Kalpa* of India teaches all of the asanas (sacred postures) for Maithuna; however, it is obvious that many of these postures are inappropriate for Westerners, and others are too shocking.

Normally, the Hindustani yogi sits in the Buddha's style (with his legs crossed in Padmasana),[78] then the yogini sits on his lap and skillfully wraps her legs around his trunk. This is how yogi and yogini connect sexually, and withdraw from their sexual connection before orgasm in order to avoid seminal ejaculation.

During the Middle Ages, many Gnostics practiced the Maithuna with vestal virgins, calling this marvelous practice *virgine subintroductis* (Sexual Magic). The *virgine subintroductis* with vestal virgins was formidable. It was practiced in the form of Karezza, so that the vestals retained their virginity. In this excellent practice, the man and the priestess lay on their sides, making sexual contact. The man introduced his phallus gradually, with extreme caution, between the vaginal labia and the hymen. With time the hymen became elastic, thus enabling deeper penetrations each time. Thus, this is how vestals never lost their virginity; they remained virgins for their entire life. The man attained realization raising Kundalini through the spinal canal with a virgin vestal.

By means of Maithuna, man and woman assimilate each other, thus reaching the hermaphroditic, divine state of the Elohim, the teleios anthropos.[79]

The best asana (sacred posture) for Maithuna is chest to chest, face to face, solar plexus to solar plexus, in order to form a perfect androgyny, with man and woman withdrawing from the sexual act without orgasm or seminal ejaculation.

---

78 Seated, cross-legged position. "Sit on the ground by spreading the legs forward. Then place the right foot on the left thigh and the left foot on the right thigh. Place the hands on the knee-joints. You can make a fingerlock and keep the locked hands over the left ankle. This is very convenient for some persons. Or you can place the left hand over the left knee and then place the right hand over the right knee with the palm facing upwards and the index finger touching the middle portion of the thumb (Chinmudra)." —Swami Sivananda.

79 Greek, a completed human being, having reached fulfillment of the goal.

Pseudo-esoteric and pseudo-occult reactionaries suppose that they can awaken Kundalini by means of brahmacharya or forced celibacy. All initiates of authentic schools of mysteries know through direct experience that without Tantric practices it is impossible to achieve the awakening and development of the seven grades of the power of fire.

There are two types of brahmacharya (sexual abstention):

- Solar brahmacharya
- Lunar brahmacharya

Solar brahmacharya is obligatory for all those who have already been born in the superior worlds with solar bodies–that is, for those who have left the Ninth Sphere.

Lunar brahmacharya is practiced by many sincere but mistaken people, by many ignoramuses who have never worked in the Ninth Sphere, who have not built the solar bodies, who are without inner Self-realization. The practice of lunar brahmacharya–in other words, the sexual abstention of those who have not built the solar bodies–is harmful because they become charged with frightfully malignant and terrible vibrations.

Let us understand that these frightfully malignant and terrible vibrations are the Poisonioonoskirian vibrations or lunar, centrifugal sexual forces. These types of tenebrous vibrations generally awaken the Kundabuffer organ.

It is commendable to know that when the serpent (lunar, centrifugal sexual forces) precipitates from the coccyx downward, it is transformed into the tail of Satan, the abominable Kundabuffer organ.

Lunar brahmacharya, with its terrible and malignant Poisonioonoskirian vibrations originates bigotry and expert cynicism of the highest degree.

Degenerate infrasexuals hate and condemn Gnostics because we teach the mysteries of sex; however, they are never scandalized by their own lasciviousness, adultery, fornication, etc.

Whosoever wants to attain the realization of their Being without Maithuna (Sexual Magic) is a definite candidate for the infernal worlds of the submerged mineral kingdom.

There are three types of Tantra:[80]

- White
- Black
- Grey

In white Tantra, ejaculation of the semen is prohibited.

In black Tantra, ejaculation of the semen is obligatory.

In grey Tantra, ejaculation of the semen is not considered important, yet in the long run, grey Tantra is transformed into black Tantra.

In white Tantra, the serpent ascends along the length of the medulla of the spinal cord.

In black Tantra, the serpent descends, projecting itself down from the coccyx towards the atomic infernos of the human being, thus becoming Satan's tail.

Kundalini has seven degrees of power of fire. Only by practicing Maithuna daily over a period of twenty or thirty years can a person achieve the total development of Kundalini.

The falling serpent, the Kundabuffer organ, develops the inferior chakras of the lower abdomen and transforms the human being into a terribly perverse and malignant beast.

The serpent ascending through the medullar canal of the dorsal spine develops all the divine powers of the human being. Devi Kundalini, the igneous serpent of our magical powers, is Isis, Adonia, Rhea, Cybele, Tonantzin, Mary, etc.

The solar bodies are gestated within the womb of Devi Kundalini, the Divine Mother. When the initiates are born from the womb of the Divine Mother in the superior worlds, when they leave the Ninth Sphere (sex), it is forbidden for them to ever return into the Ninth Sphere (sex) again.

The Twice-born enter a secret temple, and if they were to have sex again, they would fall, losing all their powers.

Every initiate who reaches the Second Birth—about which Jesus spoke to Nicodemus—faces the problem of disintegrat-

80 The word Tantra here is not limited to those groups who use the word; rather, it indicates all religions and spiritual groups. For instance, there are very popular Taoist practices that never mention the word Tantra, but they promote sexual practices that are obviously black.

ing the ego or pluralized "I" and the elimination of the lunar bodies. If the initiate does not accomplish the elimination of the pluralized "I" and the lunar bodies, one is transformed into a hasnamuss[81] with a double center of gravity.

The secret master (dressed in solar bodies) and the pluralized "I" (dressed in lunar bodies) constitute a double personality, a very serious problem that needs to be resolved. Every hasnamuss has two inner personalities: one is solar and the other is lunar. Thus, if newborn masters do not want to become hasnamussen, they must eliminate their inner lunar personality.

Amongst the most remarkable hasnamussen, we have the case of Andrameleck. There is Andrameleck the white magician, and Andrameleck the terrible and frightful black magician. Although they are quite distinct and different, they constitute one individual. It is clear that the tenebrous Andrameleck will have to devolve within the submerged mineral kingdom until becoming dust. Only in that manner can the Essence, the Buddhata, the soul, be liberated in order to return to the white Andrameleck, the secret master.

The newborn master with solar bodies must love, adore, worship their Mother Kundalini. Only She can help us eliminate the various entities that in their conjunction constitute the pluralized "I."

In the internal worlds every newborn master is subjected to many esoteric tests. These kinds of tests allow the newborn master to know in depth all the subconscious, submerged entities, which come from a remote past, and which constitute one's pluralized "I." Yet, only the Divine Mother can eliminate from the lunar bodies those tenebrous entities,

---

81 A term used by Gurdjieff in reference to a person with a divided consciousness: part of it is free and natural, and part is trapped in the ego. In synthesis, everyone who has ego is a hasnamuss, yet there are four basic types, of increasing danger:

- mortal: the common person
- those with the solar astral body
- those with the solar bodies created
- fallen angels

which personify our secret defects and which come from a remote past. For that the initiate must comprehend in depth, in all the levels of the mind, every defect.

Thus, it is necessary to know that the mind cannot reduce any defect to cosmic dust. The only thing that the mind can do is to control the defects, to hide them from itself, to pass them from one level into another, etc. The changes attained by the mind are very superficial; they are useless. We need radical and profound changes, and these are possible only with the help of our Mother Kundalini, the igneous serpent of our magical powers.

Within the different unconscious and infra-conscious, etc. levels of the initiate's own mind, one has entities that perform actions totally opposite to the actions that one is accustomed to do. These strange, submerged entities, located within one's lunar bodies, are frightful fornicators, adulterous, criminal, and perverse. They are not, however, imprisoned inside the lunar bodies, since they can leave or enter the lunar bodies; they can travel and project themselves into the molecular regions of nature.

If during meditation the initiate is trying to understand, for example, the defect of lust in order to eliminate it, then during one's chores in the internal worlds one can be doing the opposite, fornicating and committing adultery. These kinds of entities act in the submerged, subconscious regions in an independent manner, far from our reasoning and willpower; however, they are not foreign or strange entities, these are "myself," "my self-willed."

Any newborn master suffers the unspeakable because one cannot control these subconscious parts of oneself, that is, these submerged, infra-conscious, unconscious, etc., entities; thus, one's only remedy is to beseech, ask, and clamor for help from our Mother Kundalini, the sacred serpent.

There is a cosmic didactic in regards to this subject, which are esoteric tests. The initiate is repeatedly subjected to a certain test, thus, if one fails, then it is necessary to cry out, to beg for help from one's Mother Kundalini, to beseech one's sacred serpent to extract from within—to eliminate from one's

Durga, a Hindu symbol of the power of the Divine Mother Kundalini to conquer the demon ego.

"I take refuge in the Divine Mother Durga,
Who shines like a fire due to her penances,
Who resides in actions and their fruits and makes them effective,
And I salute her who helps us cross our difficulties."
—Maha Narayana Upanishad

lunar bodies—the psychological "I," or the psychological entity that personifies the defect that made one fail the test.

The initiate is submitted to many esoteric tests—some related to anger, others to greed, yet more to lust, envy, laziness, gluttony, etc., but following a particular order, a special didactic. The initiate is repeatedly placed in different circumstances, situations, and times where one does not even remotely remember one's esoteric studies or the path, etc.

The work of eliminating these entities that constitute the pluralized "I" is more bitter than bile, thus in these tests, the initiate suffers the unspeakable, because in the subconscious, unconscious, and infra-conscious regions, the initiate ends up fornicating, adulterating, committing crimes, which in the physical world one would never commit, not even for the all the gold in the world.

So, only the Mother Kundalini, only the Divine Mother, can help the initiate in this work of casting submerged entities into the infernal worlds.

When the lunar bodies become emptied, when the pluralized "I" no longer inhabits them, then the initiate enters into a mystic trance; one remains in the internal worlds for three days. During these three days, one's body remains comatose. When one returns to the physical body, one no longer has lunar bodies, but solar bodies. The superior adepts help one to get rid of those lunar vehicles, which gradually disintegrate in the molecular world.

The initiate, with only solar bodies, is totally self-realized; one is a master of the day, a master of the mahamanvantara, with power over life and death, and over all that is, all that has been, and all that shall be.

Whosoever has studied the history of magic knows very well what has been stated in all epochs regarding all great initiates who were dead for three days and thereafter they resurrected on the third day.

In certain secret temples, a spear was laid on the mystic's chest, and one fell into a trance. For the resurrection, after three days, the body was positioned with the head towards the East. What the initiate learned in the internal worlds during those three days corresponds to the mysteries.

Chapter 12

Opium, the "I," the Subconsciousness

Opium has more than four hundred active elements, yet chemists only know forty-two elements. Here we mention these forty-two elements that are named:

Morphine	Tiktoutine	Kolomonine
Protopine	Kolotine	Koilononine
Lanthopine	Xanthaline	Cotarmine
Porphyroine	Zoutine	Hydrocotarmine
Opium or narcotine	Tritopine	Opianine or meconine
Paramorphine or thebaine	Laudanine	Meconoiozine
Phormine or pseudomorphine	Laudanosine	Listotorine
Metamorphine	Podotorine	Phyktonosine
Gnoscopine	Arkhatosine	Codeine
Oleopine	Tokitosine	Narceine
Atropine	Liktonosine	Pseudocodeine
Pirotine	Meconidine	Microparaine
Rheadine	Papaverine	Microthebaine
	Cryptonine	Messaine
	Kadminine	

Generally, opium or some of its active elements are usually used by drug addicts and all type of vicious people in order to fortify the awful consequences of the abominable Kundabuffer organ (tail of Satan).[82]

It is commendable to know that in the remote past all human beings developed the abominable Kundabuffer organ (tail of Satan) due to a lamentable mistake of certain sacred individuals. Later, those sacred individuals removed the abominable Kundabuffer organ from humanity by intelligently storing the sacred fire within the coccygeal chakra (church of Ephesus, Muladhara chakra), the magnetic center located in the coccygeal bone at the base of the dorsal spine. The awful consequences of the Kundabuffer organ are constituted

82 Originally a useful organ that served the function of helping ancient humanity become focused on material, physical existence, it became corrupted by desire and the sexual fall, thus resulting in the emergence of the ego and the fortification of the sexual energy in a negative polarity, and has since been symbolized by the tail of the devils, the tail of Satan. Read *The Elimination of Satan's Tail* by Samael Aun Weor.

by that legion of devils that any person carries within their lunar bodies.

Mendelejeff intelligently reunited and listed all the names of the active elements of opium, classifying them according to their atomic weight.

The sacred law of the Heptaparaparshinokh, the law of seven, governs the seven fundamental, basic crystallizations of opium.

It is commendable to know that seven basic crystallizations correspond to the seven basic crystallizations of the opium, and another seven to those seven, thus becoming 49 basic crystallizations, which are unknown by the official science.

The seven independent properties of opium—the seven fundamental crystallizations—have seven defined, subjective properties that correspond to seven subjective states of the human subconsciousness.

The seven-times-seven crystallizations of opium correspond with seven-times-seven subjective states of opium, and with seven-times-seven subconscious states of the human being.

In our earlier 1965-1966 message,[83] we spoke widely about opium in relation with colors and sounds. Today, our only purpose is to study the relationship of opium with the subjective states and the human subconsciousness.

If we want to destroy the awful consequences of the abominable Kundabuffer organ within ourselves, first we need to comprehend that those awful consequences are processed in each one of the forty-nine subconscious levels of the human being.

It is necessary to clarify that within those forty-nine subconscious states of the human being we include the so-called infra-conscious, unconscious states etc.

All the small devils or "I's" that are created within the five cylinders of the human machine are the awful consequences of the abominable Kundabuffer organ.

We have already stated and we repeat again: the five cylinders of the human machine are the intellect, emotion, movement, instinct, and sex.

83 *Spiritual Power of Sound* by Samael Aun Weor.

To our disgrace, the awful consequences of the abominable Kundabuffer organ remain in these five cylinders of the human machine.

The vicious opium people, the drug addicts, unfortunately fortify the awful consequences of the abominable Kundabuffer organ within the five cylinders of their human machines.

The little "I's" that in their conjunction constitute that which is called ego, "I," myself, self-willed, live within the forty nine levels of the human subconsciousness.

The atomic material is different in each of the forty-nine subconscious levels of the human being.

The psychological state is distinct, different, in each of the forty-nine levels or regions of the human subconsciousness.

Any defect can disappear from the intellectual region, however, despite that fact, this does not signify that the demon that personifies it has ceased to exist; that demon, like the defect which characterizes it, continues to exist as a second unit in the second subconscious region. Likewise, any defect can disappear from the second subconscious region, yet it continues to exist as a third unit in the third subconscious region, and so on, successively.

There are seven primary units, and there are seven secondary subconscious units within the seven primary units. Likewise, there are seven tertiary independent units within the seven secondary subconscious units. There are also processes of mutual relation, mutual influence, etc., in all of this.

This explains the reason for the didactics in cosmic tests: if an initiate is victorious in a certain test of lust in the physical world, he can fail in the same test at the secondary or tertiary subconscious unit. An initiate can be victorious in tests of lust in 48 subconscious regions, yet fail in the forty-ninth region.

The initiate's different entities or "I's" that inhabit the forty-nine regions–which correspond to the forty-nine subjective states of opium–usually commit crimes which horrify, even when the initiate is entirely a saint in the physical world.

The subconscious entities or "I's" that constitute the ego are truly independent demons who have robbed part of our consciousness and who do quite the contrary to what we will.

If in this physical world we decide not to fornicate, then in the secondary, tertiary, quaternary subconscious, etc., regions we do exactly the opposite. In these subconscious regions, initiates fornicate even when in the physical world they have reached perfect chastity.

What is most grave is the state of self-independence whereupon those subconscious submerged "I's" act and live.

What is most grave is to not be able to say, "Those entities are something strange, different," since indeed those entities are me, myself.

When tested in this or that defect, many initiates are victorious in thirty or forty regions, yet in the other subconscious regions they fail lamentably.

It is evident that our defects will continue to exist as long as those subconscious, submerged entities continue to exist in our forty-nine subconscious regions.

It is urgent to comprehend each defect, not only in the intellectual level, but also in each of the forty-nine subconscious departments of the mind.

Moreover, the most grave problem arises in us when—in spite of having comprehended a defect in all forty-nine subconscious levels of the mind—we fail when submitted to the test. That failed test indicates to us that we still have the defect that we want to annihilate.

It is evident that if the "I" that personifies the defect that we want to disintegrate continues to exist within any subconscious region, the outcome of the tests is failure.

Thus, in this case, only the Mother Kundalini, the igneous serpent of our magical powers, can help us. She can extract, remove from our lunar bodies, the defect in itself—that is to say, the "I" that personifies it. So, without the Divine Mother it is impossible to extract the hidden defects—personified in small, submerged, subconscious "I's"—from the deep subconscious regions.

Kundalini is a compound word formed by the union of two: "Kunda" that reminds us of the abominable Kundabuffer organ, and "Lini" which signifies "to cease." Thus, Kundalini means "the ceasing of the Kundabuffer organ." The Kundalini ends the awful consequences of the abominable Kundabuffer organ.

We already stated and we repeat again that the awful consequences of the tenebrous Kundabuffer organ are personified in the pluralized "I."

Whosoever wants to dissolve the pluralized "I" must let go of self-esteem and the over-consideration of their self, since those who live very attached to themselves, those who love themselves too much, will never be able to dissolve their pluralized "I."

Practical life, social gatherings, become a full-sized mirror where we can discover ourselves. In social gatherings, our hidden defects surface from within, they arise spontaneously, and if we are in a state of alertness, we then see them, we discover them.

Any hidden defect must be placed under terrifying intellectual analyses, and after having deeply comprehended it intellectually, then it is necessary to investigate and comprehend it in all the levels of the mind, of the subconsciousness, by means of meditation. This comprehension leads initiates to subconscious regions where we are like leaves blown by the wind. Then, impotent, incapable of eliminating the discovered defect, we need to ask the Divine Mother Kundalini for her assistance. Only She can extract the demon who personifies that defect from our subconscious depths. Thus, she helps us by casting into the infernal worlds the submerged entity that personifies the defect that we want to reduce to dust. With the assistance of the Divine Mother Kundalini, the submerged subconscious entities, components of our defects, must little by little enter into the infernal worlds.

People covet virtues, without comprehending that any type of coveting fortifies the pluralized "I." Thus, there are many people who deceive themselves by coveting to not be covetous.

There are many people who covet the virtue of kindness. Those wretched people do not want to comprehend that the virtue of kindness is born within us only by comprehending all of the processes of anger in all of our subconscious departments.

There are many people who covet the virtue of chastity. Those wretched people do not want to understand that the virtue of chastity is born within us only by comprehending all of the processes of lust in all the subconscious departments.

Pride is usually disguised in the tunic of humility, thus there are many people who covet the virtue of humility, without comprehending that only by making a dissection of pride in all of the subconscious levels of the mind is the exotic flower of humility born in us in a natural and simple manner.

Envy is the secret trigger of any social machinery, thus there are many people who covet the virtue of happiness for their neighbor's well-being, yet those people do not want to understand that only by comprehending the infinite processes of envy in all of the subconscious departments of the mind is the virtue of joy for our neighbor's well-being born within us.

Many lethargic people covet the virtue of diligence, but they do not want to understand that only by comprehending the processes of laziness in all of the levels of the mind is diligence, activity, born in us.

Many gluttons covet the virtue of temperance, of sobriety, but they do not want to realize that only by comprehending the processes of gluttony in the different corridors and turnabouts of the mind is the necessity of eating little and being moderate in drinking born in us in a natural and spontaneous manner.

Anger usually is disguised with the gown of the judge or with a bitter smile.

There are many people who do not covet money, social position, etc., but they covet virtues, honors, paradise, psychic powers, etc.

There are terrifically chaste people in the intellectual level, but are frightful fornicators in the different subconscious regions. Fornication usually is disguised with the flattery given to the girl who walks on the street, or in the so-called very "serious" conversation with the person of the opposite sex, or with the pretext of devotion to beauty, etc.

There are many people who do not envy money, social status, ranks, honors, possessions, but they envy the saints, they covet their virtues so that they can also become saints.

There are people who dress humbly, nonetheless they have sublime pride, they are conceited with their simplicity; they do not boast about anything, thus they not only hide their pride from others but also from themselves.

Some gluttons disguise their gluttony with the pose of simple people that barbecue on Sundays and picnic days. Others try to justify their defect by saying that they need to feed themselves well in order to work, etc.

In the subconscious regions, each defect is multifaceted, and it is represented by multiple small, subjective entities or "I's" that live within our lunar bodies, and that project themselves within the subconscious regions or lands of the mind.

Only through in depth comprehension and with the help of the Divine Mother Kundalini can we eliminate those "I's" from our lunar bodies.

The initiate, with the aid of the Divine Mother, not only needs to eliminate desire, but moreover the shadow of desire, and even the memory of that shadow.

People confuse passion with love. In life it is very difficult to find truly legitimate love in a couple. The only thing in the world are passionate couples. Passion is disguised with the clothing of love, and recites about delights and things of paradise.

It may be that in the world there are some truly enamored couples who love and adore each other; however, we must look for this kind of case with Diogenes' lantern.[84]

---

84 (Greek Διογένης) A controversial Greek philosopher who extolled poverty as virtuous, begged for a living, and slept in a tub in the marketplace. He was notorious for his provocative and confrontational behavior, and was one of the only people to survive publicly insulting Alexander, who deeply respected Diogenes. One story relates that Diogenes walked the city carrying a lamp in the daytime, looking for a true human but not finding any.

Some passionate couples can swear that they are enamored, that they love each other, and even marry and live many years, or their whole life, convinced that they are enamored, yet are totally deceived by the poison of passion.

Common and ordinary people would hardly admit these affirmations, yet any initiate comes to know and comprehend this when they are put under rigorous tests within the different subconscious fields.

The way of the light is very narrow, contracted, and difficult; this is why it is called the path of the razor's edge.[85]

In the exoteric or public circle of humanity, there are many people who study pseudo-occultism, but among them it is very rare to find a serious person who is really resolute to work for their inner self-realization. Indeed, we have been able to demonstrate that the only thing that people are interested in is to amuse themselves, thus they have made of occultism a new form of amusement.

Everywhere abound fickle people, who like curious butterflies flutter today in one school and tomorrow in another; today they listen to one lecturer and tomorrow another; today they are enthused with this teaching and tomorrow with another.

All of the fickle butterfly-people we have known waste their time lamentably, and die without having reached their self-realization.

There is an accumulative center within the mind that only wants to accumulate theories, data, amusements, etc. This center is the pluralized "I."

The different entities that form the pluralized "I" enjoy accumulating. They want to amuse themselves. Thus, when one of those entities becomes enthused by the path of the razor's edge, it is soon displaced by another entity that does not want anything to do with this path, and then we see that person enter another school, thus abandoning the path.

The pluralized "I" is the worst enemy of the realization of the inner Self. What is most grave is the subtle form of

---

85 "A sharpened razor's edge is hard to cross – The dangers of the path–wise seers proclaim them!" –Katha Upanishad 3:14

self-deceit, since whosoever leaves the path of the razor's edge firmly believes to have left the error and to have found the true path.

Therefore, the Gnostic students who truly want to acquire a permanent center of consciousness[86] in order to have continuity of purpose and to attain the realization of the Inner Self must dissolve the pluralized "I." That is, they must eliminate from their lunar bodies all of the different subconscious submerged entities that we create from moment to moment within the five cylinders of the organic machine.

Only by de-egotizing ourselves do we individualize our psyche, and only by possessing true individuality do we stop flying around like curious butterflies, thus we acquire seriousness and continuity of purpose.

It is necessary to let go of the mystical pride of believing ourselves to be saints, because in this world it is very difficult to find a saint. All of us have the same defects, and those who do not have a certain defect in one direction have it in another. All of us are cut with the same scissors.

We must not forget the inner relation between the forty-nine subconscious states of opium and the forty-nine subjective states of the intellectual animal mistakenly called human being.

Nature speaks everywhere, thus the seven-times-seven subjective states of opium are also found within the human being.

We need to reduce the "I" to dust, and this is only possible by means of a basic, in depth comprehension, and with the aid of the Divine Mother Kundalini, the igneous serpent of our magical powers.

---

86 "As the pluralized 'I' dies from moment to moment, the [liberated] psychic material accumulates within us, thus becoming a Permanent Center of Consciousness... Such a marvelous center is the soul." —Samael Aun Weor, *Revolution of the Dialectic*

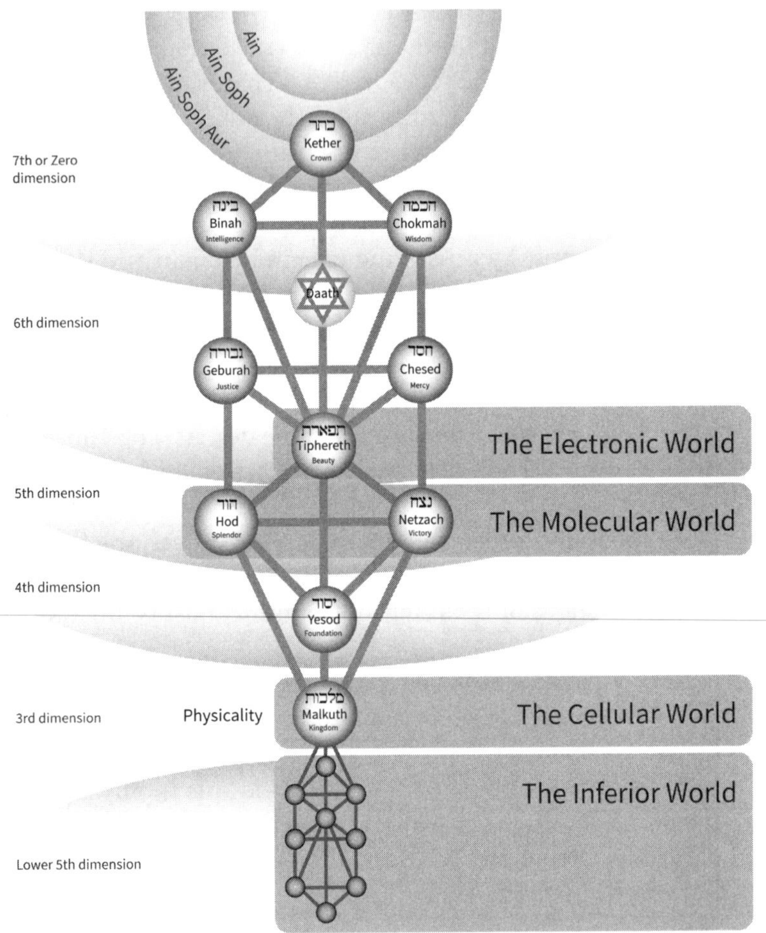

Four States of Matter on the Tree of Life

Chapter 13

Buddha's Necklace

The *Tibetan Book of the Dead*[87] states:

> *At the moment of death, the four sounds called 'awe-inspiring sounds' are heard: from the vital-force of the earth-element, a sound like the crumbling down of a mountain; from the vital-force of the water-element, a sound like the breaking of ocean waves; from the vital force of the fire-element, a sound as of a jungle afire; from the vital-force of the air-element, a sound like a thousand thunders reverberating simultaneously. The place that one getteth into in fleeing from these sounds is the womb.*

The common and ordinary intellectual state of daily life is not everything; the *Tibetan Book of the Dead* states:

> *O nobly-born, listen with full attention, without being distracted: There are six states of Bardo,*[88] *namely: the natural state of Bardo while in the womb; the Bardo of the dream-state; the Bardo of ecstatic equilibrium, while in deep meditation; the Bardo of the moment of death; the Bardo of equilibrium during the experiencing of Reality; the Bardo of the inverse process of sangsaric existence [retrospective recapitulation of the life that just passed]. These are the six.*

Tibetan initiates intelligently define with the exotic term Bardo six different states of consciousness that are distinct from the common and ordinary, routine, intellectual state of daily life.

---

87 The actual title is "The Great Book of Natural Liberation through Understanding in the Between" by Padmasambhava, written down by his primary student and consort Yeshe Tsogyal, buried in the Gampo hills in central Tibet in the 8th century, and subsequently discovered by a Tibetan terton in the 14th century.

88 Tibetan; Sanskrit: antarabhava. Literally, "between."

Anyone who dies has to experience three Bardos: the Bardo of the moment of death, the Bardo of the experience of reality, and the Bardo impelling results in rebirth.

There are four states of matter within which all the mysteries of life and death are developed. There are four circles, four regions, within which are represented all the worlds and times of matter in a mineral [atomic] state, matter in a molecular state, and matter in an electronic state. These are the four ancient worlds: hell, earth, paradise, and heaven.

Every disembodied soul must strive to attain intermediate liberation in the world of free electrons, a similar state to that of a Buddha. It is urgent to know that intermediate liberation is the limitless happiness experienced between death and a new rebirth.

There are many nations or kingdoms of immense happiness in the molecular and electronic regions where, if the law of karma allows, any disembodied soul can be born internally.

During the interval between their last death and their new birth, those who have plentiful dharma[89] (addressing those people who have done very good deeds) can give themselves the luxury of some blessed vacations.

So, before their re-incorporation on the Earth, those who have done many good deeds can be born "in The Happy Western Realm, at the feet of the Buddha Amitābha, miraculously from amidst a lotus blossom" or "The Pre-eminently Happy Realm, or The Thickly-Formed Realm, or The Realm [of Those} of Long Hair," or in the kingdom of Maitreya, etc. These different kingdoms from the molecular and electronic regions glow blissfully.

There are many masters who help the defunct ones who deserve it. Those masters have methods and systems that assist the Buddhata, the Essence, the soul, in the effort to be liberated for some time from the lunar bodies and the ego, in order to enter into the kingdoms of the molecular and electronic regions.

89 Here, dharma means karmic credit owed for good actions.

It is lamentable that the Soul, the Essence, has to return into its lunar bodies, which the ego inhabits. Such a return is inevitable in order to be reborn in the physical world.

The souls that attain intermediate liberation are very few. (Do not confuse intermediate liberation with final liberation).

After physical death, any soul can ascend into the kingdoms of happiness within the molecular and electronic worlds, or descend into the infernal worlds of the mineral kingdom, or immediately or eventually enter into a new physical body in a manner similar to the one it had before. These three roads from the fateful Chinvat Bridge[90] are wisely described and with astonishing clarity in the Zoroastrian legend:

> *Everyone whose good works are three grams more than his sin, goes to Heaven; everyone whose sin is more goes to Hell; whereas he in whom both are equal, remains in the Hamistikan till the future body or resurrection.*

The law of karma—the wise law that adjusts effects to causes—is in charge of giving everyone after their death that which they deserve. The law is the law, and the law is fulfilled.

Intermediate liberation, the bliss in the kingdoms of the molecular and electronic regions, has an end; thus, once the reward is exhausted, the Essence returns into its lunar bodies where the ego dwells; thereafter, the return, the re-incorporation, the entrance into a new womb begins. The *Tibetan Book of the Dead* states:

> *Direct thy wish, and enter into the womb. At the same time, emit thy gift-waves (of grace or goodwill) upon the womb which thou art entering, (transforming it thereby) into a celestial mansion.*

In this day and age, the souls who after their physical death enter into the different kingdoms from the molecular and electronic regions are very few.

---

90 "Bridge of judgment" that separates the world of the living from the world of the dead.

Through time, the ego has become exaggeratedly strong, extremely complicated, and therefore, the Essence, the soul, is strongly imprisoned within the lunar bodies.

In these times of worldly crisis, most souls are being born in the infernal worlds (mineral kingdom) to not return, or they are immediately re-incorporated without ascending into the kingdoms of the gods.

The great law only grants one hundred and eight lives to the human being, and this reminds us of the Buddha's necklace with one hundred and eight beads.

If the human being does not know how to take advantage of the one hundred and eight beads of the Buddha's necklace, if the human being does not achieve the inner realization of one's Self during these one hundred and eight lives, one is then born within the infernal worlds of nature. Commonly, as their times expire, all human beings descend into the infernal worlds.

Many prophets, avatars, saviors, have come into the world. Comprehending the terrors of the abyss, they have wanted to save us. But humanity does not like the avatars, the saviors. Humanity is not concerned with salvation.

This matter about the inner realization of the Self is only possible based on tremendous super-efforts, yet humanity does not like super-efforts. People only say, "Let us eat and drink, since tomorrow we will die."

The inner realization of the Self can never be the outcome of any mechanicity, even an evolutionary type of mechanicity. The law of evolution and its twin sister the law of devolution are purely mechanical laws of nature that cannot realize the Self of anybody.

Whosoever wants the inner realization of their Self has to tread the path of the razor's edge, the difficult path of the revolution of the consciousness. This path is more bitter than bile. This path is disliked by everybody.

It is necessary for the secret master to be born within us. It is necessary to die; the ego must die. It is urgent to sacrifice ourselves for humanity, since that is the law of the Solar Logos; he is self-sacrificed when crucifying himself in the worlds so that all the beings can have life, and a very abundant life.

To be born is a sexual problem. To die is a matter of dissolving the "I." To sacrifice oneself on behalf of humanity is love.

This subject matter displeases people, of enduring twenty or thirty years in the ninth sphere in order to have the right to be born in the superior worlds, of psychologically dying—that is, dissolving our beloved "I"—and of sacrificing the self on behalf of humanity.

Humanity is not interested in the inner realization of the Self, thus it is evident that nothing can be given unto the one who does not want it.

To get money, to eat, to drink, to reproduce, to amuse themselves, to have power, prestige, etc.—these are the only things that people are interested in. This explains why few are those who are saved:

> *"Many are called but few are chosen."* —Matthew 22:14

In this world abound many people who apparently want the realization of their Self in order to have the right to enter into the kingdom of esotericism, nevertheless, deep down, what those people want is to amuse themselves with these studies, and that is all. Those people are curious butterflies who flutter today in one school and tomorrow in another; they do not know the path, and if they manage to find it, they get very excited in the beginning, and thereafter, when they see that the work is serious, they flee frightened, looking for refuge in another school.

The line of life is spiral, thus in each reincarnation humanity is descending the spiral staircase until arriving at the infernal worlds of the mineral kingdom.

Time is ten times longer, ten times slower, and terribly boring in the inferno (mineral kingdom); a payment of our karmic debt is made every one hundred years.

The descent into the infernal worlds is a backward journey, devolving in time, backing down through the animal, vegetal, and mineral states. When arriving at the fossil state, the egos and its lunar bodies become cosmic dust.

The soul is liberated when the ego and the lunar bodies become dust in the inferno. The soul returns to the primeval chaos, ready to evolve again, rising over several eternities through the mineral, vegetal, and animal states, until again reaching the human state.

So, the souls who do not take advantage of the one hundred and eight lives represented by the one hundred and eight beads of the Buddha's necklace are born within the infernal worlds located underneath the Earth and waters, which is the Hindu Naraka, the Babylonian Aralu, the Earth of No-return, the region of dense darkness, the house whose inhabitants do not see the light, the region where dust is their bread and their food mud. The inferno is the melting crucible, where the rigid forms, the lunar bodies and the ego, must be melted, reduced to dust, so that the soul is liberated.

The time that the soul has to live within the infernal worlds depends on its karma. It is obvious that those terrible black magicians who developed the Kundabuffer organ and chakras of the lower abdomen, the Lucifers, Anagarikas, Ahrimans, etc., live entire eternities, complete mahamanvantaras, within those infernal regions, before becoming cosmic dust.

Common and ordinary people, the everyday people, those who did not realize their Self because they were not interested in self-realization, but who were not decidedly perverse, only last within the infernal worlds about eight hundred to one thousand years.

Severe punishments are given to those who dishonored the gods, the fallen bodhisattvas, the hasnamussen with double centers of gravity, and for those parricidal and matricidal ones, and for the assassins and people of war and masters of black magic. The *Tibetan Book of the Dead* states:

> *Falling therein, thou wilt have to endure unbearable misery, whence there is no certain time of getting out.*

Into the infernal worlds enter not only the decisively perverse, but also those who already lived their one hundred and eight lives and did not attain realization:

> *Every tree therefore which bringeth not forth good fruit is hewn down, and cast into the fire.* –Luke 3:9

Theosophists state that there are three paths of perfection, and Annie Besant wrote about these three paths. The three paths receive the names of Karma Yoga, Jnana Yoga, Bhakti Yoga.

Karma Yoga is the path of upright action.

Jnana Yoga is the path of the mind.

Bhakti Yoga is the path of devotion.

Through Karma Yoga we live uprightly, harvesting plenty of Dharma (reward), but we do not create the solar bodies with it because creation is a sexual problem.

Through Jnana Yoga we become skillful in meditation and yoga, but we do not create the solar bodies because this creative work is made with the sexual hydrogen Si-12.

Through Bhakti Yoga we can tread the devotional path and reach ecstasy, but this does not signify the creation of the solar bodies.

There are schools that affirm there are seven paths, and there are other schools that state that there are twelve paths. Jesus the Christ said:

> *Enter ye in at the strait gate: for wide is the gate, and broad is the way, that leadeth to destruction, and many there be which go in thereat: Because strait is the gate, and narrow is the way, which leadeth unto life, and few there be that find it.* –Matthew 7:13, 14

Never, ever did the Master of Masters say that there were three gates or three ways. He only spoke of a single door and a single way. So, from where have they taken that there are three paths of liberation? From where have these schools taken that there are seven gates or paths for liberation? From where did these pseudo-occultist and pseudo-esoteric organizations take that there are twelve paths?

Indeed, there is only a single path and a single gate. No human being knows more than Christ, and he never spoke about three, neither of seven, nor of twelve paths.

The path has much of Karma, Jnana and Bhakti Yoga, it has much of the seven yogas, but there is only one single, narrow, strait, and frightfully difficult path.

The path is different; it is opposed to our everyday, routine life. The path is one hundred percent revolutionary; it is against everything and everybody. The path is more bitter than bile. It is the path of the revolution of the consciousness with its three factors, namely, to be born, to die, and to sacrifice oneself on behalf of humanity. Through this path the wretched intellectual animal must become a different being.

Those who find the path are very rare, and those who do not abandon the path are even rarer. Indeed, not all can be developed as human beings and become different. Even though this seems an injustice, deep down it is not; given that people do not wish it, people are not interested in becoming different, and therefore, a thing must not be given unto the one who does not want it, who does not wish it, who is not interested in it.

Why should people be given what they do not want? If the wretched intellectual animals mistakenly called humans were forced to become different beings, when they are satisfied with what they are, then this indeed would be a great injustice.

It is clear that everything in nature is submitted to the law of number, measurement, and weight. All human beings have one hundred and eight lives, and if they do not know how to take advantage of them, the time expires and the entrance into the infernal worlds becomes inevitable.

The realization of the inner Self of the human being can never be the outcome of the mechanical evolution of nature, but the fruit of tremendous super-efforts. Yet, sadly, humanity does not like super-efforts.

Chapter 14
Gnosis

Let us now study a chapter of the Chinese gospel called the Tao, with the purpose of once again clarifying our Gnostic doctrine.

> *Chao Hsiang Tzu led out a company of a hundred thousand men to hunt in the Central Mountains. Lighting the dry undergrowth, they set fire to the whole forest, and the glow of the flames was visible for a hundred miles around. Suddenly a man appeared, emerging from a rocky cliff (that is to say, passing miraculously out of the actual stone itself), and was seen to hover in the air amidst the flames and the smoke. Everybody took him for a disembodied spirit. When the fire had passed, he walked quietly out, and showed no trace of having been through the ordeal. Hsiang Tzu marveled thereat, and detained him for the purpose of careful examination. In bodily form he was undoubtedly a man, possessing the seven channels of sense, besides which his breathing and his voice also proclaimed him a man. So the prince inquired what secret power it was that enabled him to dwell in rock and to walk through fire.*
>
> *"'What do you mean by rock? What do you mean by fire?' replied the man.*
>
> *Hsiang Tzu said, "What you just now came out of is rock; what you just now walked through is fire."*
>
> *"I know nothing of them," replied the man.*
>
> *The incident came to the ears of Marquis Wên of the Wei State, who spoke to Tzu Hsia about it, saying: "What an extraordinary man this must be!"*
>
> *"From what I have heard the Master say," replied Tzu Hsia, "the man who achieves harmony with Tao enters into close unison with external objects, and none of*

> *them has the power to harm or hinder him. Passing through solid metal or stone, walking in the midst of fire or on the surface of water—all these things become possible to him."*
>
> *"Why, my friend," asked the Marquis, "cannot you do all this?'"*
>
> *"I have not yet succeeded," said Tzu Hsia, "in cleansing my heart of impurities and discarding (false) wisdom. I can only find leisure to discuss the matter in tentative fashion."*
>
> *"And why," pursued the Marquis, "does not the Master himself perform these feats?"*
>
> *"The Master," replied Tzu Hsia, "is is able to do these things, but he is also able to refrain from doing them," an answer that greatly delighted the Marquis.* —The Book of Lieh-Tzü by Lieh-Tzü

It is urgent to ignite the sacred fire in the central mountain range—that is to say, the dorsal spine. The Mother Kundalini gives the initiate extraordinary powers over the flaming fire, the air, the waters, and the earth.

"What do you mean by rock?" This reminds us of the Philosophical Stone of ancient Medieval alchemists. This reminds us of the doctrine of Peter. Petrous means stone, Peter, one of the twelve apostles of Christ whose birth we celebrate on this Christmas Eve.

The doctrine of Peter is the doctrine of sex, the science of Maithuna (Sexual Magic). The living stone is sex, the boulder, the rock upon which we must build the inner temple for the Inner Christ, our Lord.

Peter said,

> *Behold, I lay in Sion a chief corner stone, elect, precious: and he that believeth on him shall not be confounded. Unto you therefore which believe he is precious: but unto them which be disobedient, the stone which the builders disallowed, the same is made the head of the corner, and a stone of stumbling, and a rock of offence.* —1 Peter 2:6-8

Whosoever ignites a bonfire in the central mountain range (the dorsal spine) builds the temple (creates the solar bodies) and enters in harmony with the TAO (incarnates the Being).

Jesus Christ, whose nativity we celebrate on the eve of December 25, said,

> *Therefore whosoever hears these sayings of mine, and does them, I will liken him to a wise man, which built his house on a rock (sex): And the rain descended, and the floods came, and the winds blew, and beat on that house; and it fell not: for it was founded on a rock (sex).*
>
> *And every one that hears these sayings of mine, and does them not, shall be likened to a foolish man, which built his house on the sand (all type of theories, all kinds of practices, with total exclusion of Maithuna or Sexual Magic).*
>
> *And the rain descended, and the floods came, and the winds blew, and beat on that house; and it fell: and great was the fall of it (falling into the abyss).*
> —Matthew 7:24-27

Millions of people in the world build on the sand and hate Maithuna (Sexual Magic). They do not want to build on the rock, the stone (sex). They build on the sand of their theories, schools, etc., and believe that they are doing very well. Those wretched people are sincere and with very good intentions, but are mistaken, therefore they will fall into the abyss.

All masters who are born in the superior worlds must reduce their ego to dust, in order to liberate themselves from their lunar bodies and thus exercise the entire priesthood power of high magic, because the master (Chesed) who has not dissolved the pluralized "I," the master (Innermost) who has not eliminated the lunar bodies, still cannot exercise the priesthood power [of high magic], because he "has not yet succeeded in cleansing his heart of impurities and discarding (false) wisdom." (Tzu Hsia)

Jesus said unto his disciples:

"Cease not to seek day and night and remit not yourselves until ye find the mysteries of the Light-kingdom, which will purify you and make you into refined light and lead you into the Light-kingdom.

"Say unto them: Renounce the whole world and the whole matter therein and all its cares and all its sins, in a word all its associations which are in it, that ye may be worthy of the mysteries of the Light and be saved from all the chastisements which are in the judgments.

"Say unto them: Renounce murmuring [gossip], that ye may be worthy of the mysteries of the Light and be saved from the fire of the dog-faced [one].

"Say unto them: Renounce eavesdropping, that ye may [be worthy of the mysteries of the Light] and be saved from the judgments of the dog faced [one].

"Say unto them: Renounce litigiousness, that ye may be worthy of the mysteries of the Light and be saved from the chastisements of Ariel.

"Say unto them: Renounce false slander, that ye may be worthy of the mysteries of the Light and be saved from the fire-rivers of the dog-faced [one].

"Say unto them: Renounce false witness, that ye may be worthy of the mysteries of the Light and that ye may escape and be saved from the fire rivers of the dog-faced [one].

"Say unto them: Renounce pride and haughtiness, that ye may be worthy of the mysteries of the Light and be saved from the fire-pits of Ariel.

"Say unto them: Renounce belly-love [gluttony], that ye may be worthy of the mysteries of the Light and saved from the judgments of Amente (mineral kingdom).

"Say unto them: Renounce babbling (intellectual gibberish without spirituality), that ye may be worthy of the mysteries of the Light and be saved from the Amente.

"Say unto them: Renounce craftiness that ye may be worth of the mysteries of the Light and be saved from the chastisements which are in Amente.

"Say unto them: Renounce avarice, that ye may be worthy of the mysteries of the Light and be saved from the fire-rivers of the dog-faced [one].

"Say unto them: Renounce love of the world, that ye may be worthy of the mysteries of the Light and be saved from the pitch and fire-coats of the dog-faced [one].

"Say unto them: Renounce pillaging [taking what is not yours], that ye may be worthy of the mysteries of the Light and be saved from the fire-rivers of Ariel.

"Say unto them: Renounce evil conversation, that ye may be worthy of the mysteries of the Light and be saved from the chastisements of the fire rivers...

"Say unto them: Renounce wickedness, that ye may be worthy of the mysteries of the Light and be saved from the fire-seas of Ariel.

"Say unto them: Renounce pitilessness [cruelty], that ye may be worthy of the mysteries of the Light and be saved from the judgments of the dragon-faced [ones].

"Say unto them: Renounce wrath [anger], that ye may be worthy of the mysteries of the Light and be saved from the fire-rivers of the dragon-faced [ones].

"Say unto them: Renounce cursing, that ye may be worthy of the mysteries of the Light and be saved from the fire-seas of the dragon-faced [ones].

"Say unto them: Renounce thieving, that ye may be worthy of the mysteries of the Light and be saved from the bubbling seas of the dragon-faced [ones.]

The Wrath of Jesus Cleansing the Temple

"Say unto them: Renounce robbery, that ye may be worthy of the mysteries of the Light and be saved from Yaldabaoth.[91]

"Say unto them: Renounce slandering, that ye may be worthy of the mysteries of the Light and be saved from the fire-rivers of the lion-faced [one].

"Say unto them: Renounce fighting and strife, that ye may be worthy of the mysteries of the Light and be saved from the seething rivers of Yaldabaoth.

"Say unto them: Renounce all unknowing, that ye may be worthy of the mysteries of the Light and be saved from the servitors of Yaldabaoth and the fire-seas.

"Say unto them: Renounce evil doing, that ye may be worthy of the mysteries of the Light and be saved from all the demons of Yaldabaoth and all his judgments.

"Say unto them: Renounce sloth, that ye may be worthy of the mysteries of the Light and be saved from the seething pitch-seas of Yaldabaoth.

"Say unto them: Renounce adultery, that ye may be worthy of the mysteries of the Light-kingdom and be saved from the sulphur and pitch-seas of the lion-faced [one].

"Say unto them: Renounce murder, that ye may be worthy of the mysteries of the Light and be saved from the crocodile-faced ruler, — this one who is in the cold, is the first chamber of the outer darkness.

"Say unto them: Renounce pitilessness and impiety, that ye may be worthy of the mysteries of the Light and be saved from the rulers of the outer darkness.

---

91 Hebrew ילדאבהות (Literally "Children of the Void," from ילדה = yalda= child; בהו = bohu = void; אבהות = abbott = fatherhood, parentage, paternity). This term has positive and negative interpretation, for there are children of the Void above (the Ain Soph, Sunyata, or Emptiness) and children of the Void below (the Abyss).

"Say unto them: Renounce atheism, that ye may be worthy of the mysteries of the Light and be saved from the howling and grinding of teeth.

"Say unto them: Renounce [magic] potions, that ye may be worthy of the mysteries of the Light and be saved from the great cold and hail of the outer darkness.

"Say unto them: Renounce blasphemy, that ye may be worthy of the mysteries of the Light and be saved from the great dragon of the outer darkness.

"Say unto them: Renounce the doctrines of error, that ye may be worthy of the mysteries of the Light and be saved from all the chastisements of the great dragon of the outer darkness.

"Say unto those who teach the doctrines of error and to every one who is instructed by them: Woe unto you, for, if ye do not repent and abandon your error, ye will go into the chastisements of the great dragon and of the outer darkness, which is exceedingly evil, and never will ye be cast [up] into the world, but will be non-existent until the end (you will enter into the Earth of No-return, the infernal worlds).

"Say unto those who abandon the doctrines of truth of the First Mystery: Woe unto you, for your chastisement is sad compared with [that of] all men. For ye will abide in the great cold and ice and hail in the midst of the dragon and of the outer darkness, and ye will never from this hour on be cast [up] into the world, but ye shall be frozen up in that region and at the dissolution of the universe ye will perish and become non-existent eternally (until they are reduced to dust within the infernal worlds of the mineral kingdom).

"Say rather to the men of the world: Be calm, that ye may receive the mysteries of the Light and go on high into the Light-kingdom.

"Say unto them: Be ye loving-unto-others, that ye may be worthy of the mysteries of the Light and go on high into the Light-kingdom.

"Say unto them: Be ye gentle, that ye may receive the mysteries of the Light and go on high into the Light-kingdom.

"Say unto them: Be ye peaceful, that ye may receive the mysteries of the Light and go on high into the Light-kingdom.

"Say unto them: Be ye merciful, that ye may receive the mysteries of the Light and go on high into the Light-kingdom.

"Say unto them: Give ye alms, that ye may receive the mysteries of the Light and go on high into the Light-kingdom.

"Say unto them: Minister unto the poor and the sick and distressed, that ye may receive the mysteries of the Light and go on high into the Light-kingdom.

"Say unto them: Be ye loving-unto-God, that ye may receive the mysteries of the Light and go on high into the Light-kingdom.

"Say unto them: Be ye righteous, that ye may receive the mysteries [of the Light] and go on high into the Light-kingdom.

"Say unto them: Be good, that ye may receive the mysteries [of the Light] and go on high into the Light-kingdom.

"Say unto them: Renounce all, that ye may receive the mysteries of the Light and go on high into the Light-kingdom.

'These are all the boundaries of the ways for those who are worthy of the mysteries of the Light.

"Unto, such, therefore, who have renounced in this renunciation, give the mysteries of the Light and hide

them not from them at all, even though they are sinners and they have been in all the sins and all the iniquities of the world, all of which I have recounted unto you, in order that they may turn and repent and be in the submission which I have just recounted unto you. Give unto them the mysteries of the Light-kingdom and hide them not from them at all; for it is because of the sinfulness that I have brought the mysteries into the world that I may forgive all their sins which they have committed from the beginning on.

"For this cause have I said unto you aforetime: 'I am not come to call the righteous.' Now, therefore, I have brought the mysteries that [their] sins may be forgiven for every one and they be received into the Light-kingdom. For the mysteries are the gift of the First Mystery, that he may wipe out the sins." —Pistis Sophia

Chapter 15

The Division of Attention

Those who have studied our Gnostic teachings, those who have studied this Christmas message, if they indeed become interested in the path of the razor's edge and the inner realization of their Being, will feel the longing to see, hear, smell, touch, and sense the great realities of the superior worlds.

Every human being can arrive to the experience of reality. Every human being has the right to great living experiences of the spirit, to know the kingdoms and nations of the molecular and electronic regions.

Every aspirant has the right to study at the feet of the master, to enter through the splendid doors of the temples of major mysteries, to converse face to face with the glowing children of the dawn of the mahamanvantara of creation; however, it is necessary to begin by awakening the consciousness.

It is impossible to be awakened in the superior worlds if here in this cellular, physical, material world the aspirant is asleep. Whosoever wants to awaken their consciousness in the internal worlds must awaken here and now in this dense world.

If the consciousness of the aspirant has not awakened here, in this physical world, much less it is awakened in the superior worlds.

Whosoever awakens their consciousness here and now awakens everywhere. Whosoever awakens their consciousness here in this physical world, in fact and by their own right becomes awakened in the superior worlds.

The first thing that is needed in order to awaken the consciousness is to know that it is asleep within us.

This matter about comprehending that one's consciousness is asleep is something very difficult, because normally all people are absolutely convinced that they are awake. When a person comprehends that one is asleep, one then initiates the process of self-awakening.

We are asserting something that nobody accepts. If it were said to any intellectual individual that he is asleep, you can be sure that he could be offended, since people are totally convinced that they are awake.

People are asleep, dreaming, while working.... They are asleep, dreaming, while driving their cars ... they are asleep, dreaming, when they get married. They are asleep, dreaming, during their life, and nevertheless, they are totally convinced that they are awake.

Whosoever wants to awaken their consciousness here and now must begin to comprehend the three subconscious factors, namely: identification, fascination, dreaming.

Any type of identification produces fascination and dreaming. I.e., you are walking on a street, when suddenly you are facing crowds lashing out in an intense, rash protest against something in front of Mr. President's palace; if you are not in a state of alertness, you become identified with the riot, you mix with the multitudes, you become fascinated, and soon the dream comes: you shout, throw stones, you do things that in other circumstances you would not do, even for a million dollars.

To forget oneself is an error of incalculable consequences. To identify oneself with something is the breaking point of stupidity, because the outcome becomes fascination and dreaming.

It is impossible for anyone to awaken their consciousness if they forget themselves, if they become identified with something.

To awaken the consciousness is impossible for those aspirants who allow themselves to become fascinated, if they fall into a dream.

The pugilist who is crossing blows with another pugilist sleeps profoundly. They are dreaming. They are totally identified with the event. They are fascinated, and if unexpectedly they awakened their consciousness, they would look in all directions and flee immediately from the ring, totally ashamed of themselves and the honorable public.

DAYDREAMING

You are traveling in any urban transportation within your city; you must get off from that urban transportation at a certain street, yet suddenly, the memory of a beloved relative comes to your mind, thus, you become identified with that memory, then fascination comes, and soon you are daydreaming... Then, suddenly you shout an exclamation, "Where am I? Damn it! ... I have passed my stop many blocks away... I should have got off in a previous stop, that street." Thus, quickly you realize that your consciousness had been absent; you then get off from that urban transportation and go back on foot to the stop where you should have gotten off.

Whosoever wants to awaken the consciousness must begin dividing the attention in three parts: subject, object, location.

> **Subject:** inner remembrance of oneself from moment to moment; not to forget oneself before any representation, any event.
>
> **Object:** not to become identified with anything, with any circumstance, to observe without becoming identified, without forgetting oneself.
>
> **Location:** to ask oneself, what place is this? To observe the place in detail, to ask oneself: Why am I in this place?

The division of attention in three parts will lead the aspirants to the awakening of their consciousness.

To want to vividly experience the great realities of the superior worlds without having awakened the consciousness here and now is to march on the path of error.

The awakening of the consciousness originates the development of the spatial sense and the experience of reality.

Chapter 16

Inner Remembering of One's Self

Even though it seems incredible, when aspirants are observing themselves they do not remember their Self.

Indeed, beyond any doubt, aspirants do not perceive their Self; they have no cognizance of their Self.

It seems inconceivable that when Gnostic aspirants self-observe their mannerisms when they laugh, speak, walk, etc., they forget their Self; this is incredible, but true.

Nevertheless, it is indispensable to exert the remembrance of our Self while we are observing ourselves. This is fundamental in order to attain the awakening of the consciousness.

Self-observing, self-knowing, without forgetting our Self, is terribly difficult, but frightfully urgent in order to attain the awakening of the consciousness.

What we are stating seems trivial to the people who ignore that they are asleep; they ignore that they do not remember their Self, not even when they look at their bodies in a full-length mirror, moreover, not even when they observe themselves in detail meticulously.

The forgetfulness of our Self, the lack of remembering of our Self, is indeed the causa causarum[92] of all human ignorance.

When any given person deeply comprehends that she cannot remember her Self, that she is not cognizant of her Self, then she is very close to the awakening of her consciousness.

We are stating something that has to be reflected upon deeply. What we are asserting here is very important, and if it is read mechanically, it is not possible to comprehend. Thus, our readers must reflect. Again, while self-observing, people are not capable of perceiving their own Self, of passing this perception from one center to another, etc.

To observe our own manner of speaking, laughing, walking, etc., without forgetting our Self, without loosing that awareness inside, is very difficult, and nevertheless basic, funda-

92 Cause of causes.

mental, in order to attain the awakening of the consciousness. The great master Ouspensky said,

> "The first impression that I felt when I made the effort of becoming cognizant of my Being—of being cognizant of my Self as "I," of telling my Self "I am walking, I am doing," of trying to keep alive this awareness of "I," of perceiving it within—was the following: thought remained asleep when I seized the "I." That is, I could not think or speak, and even the intensity of sensations diminished. Moreover, one could stay in that state for only a very short time."

It is necessary to dissolve the pluralized "I," to render it to ashes, but first we must know it, to study it within the forty-nine subconscious departments, symbolized among the Gnostics by the forty-nine demons of Yaldabaoth.

If a physician is going to extirpate a cancerous tumor, first he needs to diagnose it correctly. Likewise, if one wants to dissolve the "I," one needs to study it, to gain cognizance of it, to know it in the forty-nine subconscious departments.

During the inner remembering of our Self, in that tremendous super-effort of being cognizant of our "I," it is clear that the attention is divided, and here again we go to the subject of the division of attention. One part of attention goes, as is logical, towards the effort, and the other towards the ego or pluralized "I."

The inner remembering of our Self is something more than analysis of oneself; it is a new state that is only known through direct experience.

Every human being has had some of those moments, those states of inner remembering of the Self, perhaps at a moment of infinite terror, perhaps in childhood or during some journey, when we exclaimed, "And what am I doing here? Why am I here?"

The observation of our Self accompanied simultaneously by the inner remembering of our "I" is terribly difficult, and nevertheless indispensable in order to really know ourselves.

During meditation, the pluralized "I" is always doing the opposite. When we try to comprehend lust, our ego enjoys fornication. When we try to comprehend anger, in any of the forty-nine subconscious departments of Yaldabaoth it thunders and flashes. When we want to reduce covetousness to dust, the ego covets to not be covetous.

Inner remembering of one's Self is to become exactly aware of all those subconscious processes of "the self-willed," the ego, the pluralized "I."

To observe our way of thinking, speaking, laughing, walking, eating, feeling, etc., without forgetting one's Self, of the inner processes of one's ego, of what is happening within the forty-nine subconscious departments of Yaldabaoth, is indeed frightfully difficult, and nevertheless fundamental for the awakening of the consciousness.

Self-observation and inner remembering of one's Self starts the development of the spatial sense, which reaches its total maturity with the awakening of the consciousness.

The chakras mentioned by Mr. Leadbeater and many other authors are in relation to the spatial sense what flowers are in relation to the tree that gives them life. What is fundamental is the tree. The spatial sense is the normal function of the awakened consciousness.

Any truly awakened person can see, hear, touch, smell, and feel everything that occurs in the forty-nine subconscious departments of Yaldabaoth.

Any truly awakened person can verify through direct experience the dreams of people, can see the dreams of the people who walk on the streets, of the people who work in factories, of those who govern people, of any creature.

Any truly awakened person can see, hear, smell, really touch and feel all things from the superior worlds. Whosoever wants to experience the reality of everything that happens in the superior dimensions of space must awaken the consciousness here and now.

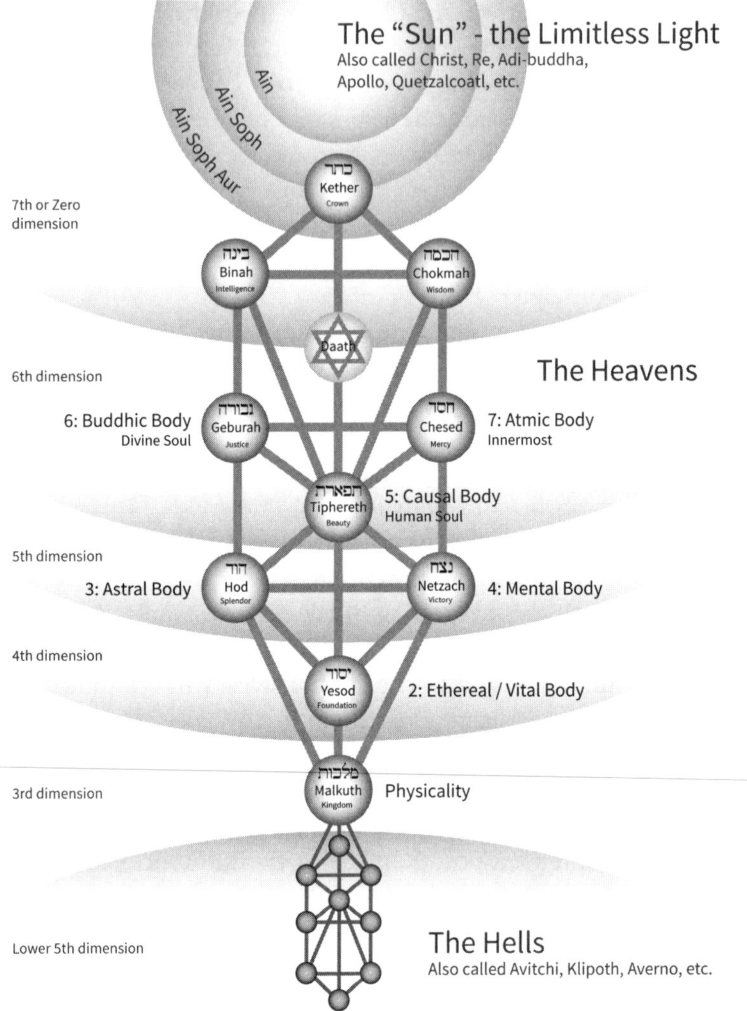

The Tree of Life of Kabbalah.

At the top is symbolized the reality of all existence, which is non-existence or Absolute Abstract Space, the Voidness or Emptiness, the Ain Soph ("limitless")

"It is the ONE LIFE, eternal, invisible, yet Omnipresent, without beginning or end, yet periodical in its regular manifestations, between which periods reigns the dark mystery of non-Being; unconscious, yet absolute Consciousness; unrealisable, yet the one self-existing reality; truly, "a chaos to the sense, a Kosmos to the reason." Its one absolute attribute, which is ITSELF, eternal, ceaseless Motion, is called in esoteric parlance the "Great Breath," which is the perpetual motion of the universe, in the sense of limitless, ever-present SPACE." —H. P. Blavatsky, The Secret Doctrine (1888)

Chapter 17

The Science of Meditation

Voidness[93] is very difficult to explain, because it is indefinable and indescribable.

> *Voidness cannot be described or expressed in words. This is because human language is created primarily to designate existent things and feelings...* –Garma C. C. Chang, The Nature of Zen

Thus, by no means is it an exaggeration to say that human languages are not adapted to describe things and feelings that are nonexistent, and nevertheless are tremendously real.

> *To attempt to discuss Voidness within the limitations of a language confined by the pattern of existence is [beyond any doubt] both futile and misleading.*
> –Garma C. C. Chang, The Nature of Zen

It is necessary to know—to experience in a living way—the illuminating aspect of the consciousness. It is urgent to feel and experience the voidness aspect of the mind.

There are two types of enlightenment: the first is usually called "dead water" because attachments remain. The second is praised as the "great life" because it is enlightenment without attachments: the Illuminating-Voidness.

In regard to enlightenment, there are degrees and degrees, rungs and rungs. First, it is necessary to attain the illuminating aspect of the consciousness, and thereafter, objective knowledge, the Illuminating-Voidness. Buddhism states:

> *...form does not differ from voidness, and voidness does not differ from form. Form is voidness and voidness is form.* –Prajnaparamita, or The Heart of Wisdom Sutra

> *...it is owing to Voidness that things can exist and, because of the very fact that things do exist, they must be Void.* –Garma C. C. Chang, The Nature of Zen

93 The fundamental reality, called Absolute, Shunyata, Brahma, Suchness, Emptiness, Illuminating Void, Ain Soph, etc.

Voidness is a clear and precise term that expresses the insubstantial and impersonal nature of beings, and an indication, a sign, of a state of an absolute absence of the pluralized "I."

Thus, only in the absolute absence of the "I" we can experience reality, that which is not of time, that which radically transforms.

> *Voidness and existence are complementary to each other and not in opposition to each other; they include and embrace, rather than exclude or negate each other.*
>
> –Garma C. C. Chang, The Nature of Zen

Common and ordinary every day people–which is people with sleeping consciousness–perceive things subjectively, namely surfaces, angles, lines. They never perceive complete bodies, namely from the inside and outside, above and below, ahead and behind, etc., and much less can they perceive the void aspect of things.

The person with an awakened consciousness and an empty and illuminated mind has eliminated the subjective elements from perception. This person perceives complete bodies, and the empty aspect of every thing. This is the non-discriminative doctrine of the middle path, the unification of voidness and existence.

The voidness is that which has no name... that which is reality... that which is the truth, thus, it does not matter what we call it. Yet, some call it Tao, others Inri, others Zen... Allah... Brahman.... Atman... God... The person who awakens the consciousness experiences the tremendous truth of no longer being a slave, and verifies with pain that the people who walk on the streets are dreaming; they "tread the streets like walking corpses."

If by means of the inner remembering of one's Self from moment to moment this awakening of the consciousness becomes continuous, one then arrives at objective consciousness, at Pure Consciousness, at the voidness aspect of the mind.

The illuminated consciousness is fundamental in order to experience reality and to reduce the pluralized "I" to cosmic dust; nevertheless, this state is still at the border of samsara[94] (the painful world in which we live).

When the initiate has arrived at the state of awakened consciousness, the initiate has taken a formidable step, but unfortunately the initiate still continues to be obfuscated by the monistic idea; the initiate is incapable of breaking the subtle threads that connect him to certain things, to certain detrimental type of effects. One has not yet arrived on the other shore.

When the initiate unties the bonds that in one or another manner tie one to the illuminating consciousness, one then reaches perfect enlightenment, reaches free and entirely insubstantial illuminating voidness.

To reach the very center of the mind, to reach the illuminated void, objective knowledge, is something tremendously difficult, but not impossible; any Gnostic can achieve it, if one works on oneself.

The illuminated voidness is not nothingness; rather, the voidness is life free in its movement. The voidness is what is, what always has been, and what always will be. The voidness is beyond time and eternity.

The mind has three hundred thousand clans or receptive centers, and each clan must vibrate at the same tone without any effort.

The mind has a feminine nature, and it is made to receive, assimilate, and comprehend. The natural state of the mind is receptive, quiet, silent, like a profound and calm ocean.

The process of thinking is an abnormal accident, whose original cause is found in the pluralized "I." When the mind is empty of all types of thoughts, when the mind is quiet, when the mind is in silence, the three hundred thousand clans vibrate to the same tone without any effort. When the mind is quiet, when the mind is in silence, then that which is reality comes unto us.

94 Sanskrit, "circling," the repeating sufferings of those who are asleep.

Buddha Shakyamuni and His Seven Serpents

Chapter 18

The Chinese Master Wu Wen

The great master Wu Wen began his meditation practices under the wise guidance of Master Tuo Weng.

> *When I first saw Master Tou Weng he taught me to work on [the koan],*[95] *"It is neither mind, nor Buddha, nor any thing." Later Yun Feng and Yueh Shan and I, with several others, vowed to help each other in our striving for the Ultimate Enlightenment. Still later I went to see Huai Shi, who taught me to work on the "Wu" word. Then I journeyed to Chang Lu, where I practiced with my companion. When I met Chin of Huai Shang, he asked me, "You have practiced for six or seven years now; what have you understood?" I answered, "Every day I just feel that there is nothing in my mind." Seeing that I had no true understanding, he asked, "From what source has your understanding been derived?" I was not sure whether I really knew the truth or not, so I dared not answer. He then said to me, "You can hold to your Work in quietness, but you lose it during activity." This alarmed me, for he had hit my weak spot. "What should one do," I inquired, "to understand this matter?" Chin answered. "Have you never heard what Chung Lao Tze said?"*
>
> *"To understand this,*
> *Face South to see the Dipper."*
>
> *Upon saying this, he left me abruptly.*
>
> *As a result I became unconscious of walking when I walked and of sitting when I sat. I put aside the*

95 "Koan" is the Japanese pronunciation of the Chinese phrase kung-an, describing a dialogue or event between Zen Master and student.

practice on the 無 "Wu"[96] *Hua Tou*[97] *for a week and concentrated my mind on trying to understand what in heaven's name he had meant by "facing South to see the Dipper." One day, when I came to the Hall of Service and sat with a group of monks, the "doubt-sensation" stuck with me and refused to dissolve. The time for dinner came and passed. Suddenly I felt my mind become bright, void, light, and transparent, my human thoughts broke into pieces like skin peeling, as if I had merged in the Void, and I saw neither person nor thing appearing before me. I returned to consciousness about half an hour later and found that my body was running with sweat. Immediately I understood the meaning of seeing the Dipper by facing South. I went to see Chin. What ever questions he put to me I could answer without hindrance or difficulty; also, I could compose stanzas freely and effortlessly. However, I still had not stripped myself to the point of reaching the state of "leaping one step upward."*

Later I went to Hsiang Yen's place in the mountains to spend the summer. The mosquitoes which infested the region bit me terribly. I had to move my hands continually to keep them away. Then I thought, "If the men in ancient times had sacrificed their bodies for the sake of Dharma, should I be afraid of mosquitoes?" With this in mind I tried to relax and endure the pests. With fists clenched and teeth tight I concentrated my mind solely on the 無 "Wu" word, bearing the continuously repeated stings of the mosquitoes with the utmost patience. Soon I felt both my mind and body sink quietly down like a house whose four walls had fallen. The state was like the Voidness; no attribute can be ascribed to it. I had sat down in the early morning,

96 Chinese 無, "wu" or "mu" has two pronunciations: one means "nothingness," and the other "Enlightenment."

97 Chinese 話頭, literally "the end of a sentence." To put one's mind into this single word ["wu"] and try to find the solution of the original question.

> *and it was not until afternoon that I arose from this period of meditation. Thereupon I knew for certain that Buddhism never misleads us or lets us down.*
>
> *Although my understanding was then quite clear, it had not yet come to the point of full maturity. I still possessed slight, subtle, hidden, and unnoticeable wrong thoughts which had not been completely exhausted.*

When Wu Wen chanted the mantra 無 WU he imitated with the U the sound of the wind in a mountain gorge, the sound of the sea when it hits the beach.

Wu Wen knew how to intelligently combine meditation with sleep. Wu Wen chanted his mantra with his mind and thought of nothing. When some desire or memory or thought arose, Wu Wen did not reject it, he studied it, analyzed it, comprehended it at all levels of the mind, and then forgot it in a radical, total or definitive way.

Wu Wen chanted his mantra in a continuous manner. He desired nothing, reasoned nothing. Any desire or thought that arose in his mind was duly comprehended and then forgotten. The chanting of the mantra was not interrupted. The mosquitoes and their stings no longer mattered.

He sat down to meditate in the early hours of the morning and only got up at sunset.

It is clear that one can enjoy meditation sitting cross-legged in the Eastern style as the Buddha did, or in the Western style in the position most comfortable, or lying down with the arms and legs open to the right and left like the five-pointed star, and with the body relaxed. Wu Wen was oriental and preferred to sit in the oriental style like the Buddha.

Until now the great Chinese master Wu Wen had managed to experience the illuminating emptiness, but something was still missing, he had not reached full maturity, in his mind there were erroneous and inadvertent thoughts, which secretly continued to exist, tempting little demons, little subconscious "I's," residues that still lived in the forty-nine subconscious apartments of Yaldabaoth.

After this experience of the illuminating void, Wu Wen went to the mountain at Kwung Chou...

> *"I meditated for six years there, for another six on the mountain of Lu Han, and for three more at Kuang Chou. Not until then did I gain my emancipation."*

At the end of these efforts and after having suffered much, Master Wu Wen achieved the final enlightenment. Master Wu Wen was a true athlete of meditation.

During his practices he understood that all mental effort creates intellectual tension and that this is harmful for meditation, because it obstructs enlightenment. Master Wu Wen never divided himself between a higher I and a lower I, because he understood that higher or lower are two sections of one same thing. Master Wu Wen felt himself, not as a god or a deva, in the style of mythomaniacs, but as an unhappy pluralized I, truly willing to die more and more within himself.

Master Wu Wen did not divide himself between me and my thoughts, because he understood that my thoughts and I are all me, and that it is necessary to be whole to achieve perfect meditation.

During meditation, Master Wu Wen was in a whole, receptive state, tremendously humble, with a still mind and in profound silence, without any kind of effort, without mental tension, without the desire to be something else, because Wu Wen knew very well that the "I" is what it is and that it can never be something more than what it is. Under these conditions, all three hundred thousand clans of Master Wu Wen's mental body vibrated intensely with the same tone, effortlessly capturing, receiving love and wisdom.

When Wu Wen was in the meditation halls and lumisials, all the monks received great benefit from the powerful vibrations of his luminous aura. Wu Wen already possessed the superior existential bodies of the Being, the solar bodies, but he needed to dissolve the "I" and achieve final illumination, and he achieved it after having suffered much.

Chapter 19

The Venustic Initiation

The Venustic Initiation is only for true human beings, never for intellectual animals.

Let "true human beings" be understood as those who already created the solar bodies. Let "intellectual animals" be understood as all of humanity, all the people who only have lunar bodies.

The Venustic Initiation is the true nativity of the tranquil heart. The Venustic Initiation is for the few; it is a grace from the Solar Logos.

In Nirvana, there are many Buddhas who–in spite of their great perfections–have never reached the Venustic Initiation.

The law of the Solar Logos is to be sacrificed on behalf of humanity. From the dawn of life, the Logos sacrifices himself. He crucifies himself in all the worlds, in every new planet that emerges into existence, so that all beings can have life, and have it in abundance.

Rare is the one who receives the Venustic Initiation. This is a very special grace. It is necessary to have previously sacrificed oneself on behalf of humanity.

Annie Besant committed the error of supposing, and even affirming, that the inner Christ, the Child God, the Savior, incarnates in the human being when one reaches the first Initiation of Major Mysteries. Annie Besant wanted to see all the cosmic drama–namely, birth, growth, death, and resurrection of Christ–in the five elementary Initiations of Major Mysteries. Annie Besant committed the error of confusing the five elementary Initiations of Fire with the Venustic Initiation.

It is necessary to know that Christ cannot be incarnated within the intellectual animal. It is urgent to comprehend that Christ, our Lord, can only be incarnated within true human beings, and that without previously having passed through the five elementary initiations of Major Mysteries, it is impossible to attain the state of authentic human.

Christ can be incarnated within us only as a grace, and after having passed through the five Initiations of Major Mysteries, and after having previously sacrificed ourselves on behalf of humanity.

That which is above is like that which is below. At the beginning of the aurora of creation, the sexual fire of the Third Logos fecundates the womb of the great mother, the fundamental substance.

The second part is performed by the Second Logos, the Cosmic Christ, by incarnating himself within the worlds that are arising, so that all beings can have life, and have it in abundance.

This event is repeated within the human microcosmos. The first one who intervenes is the Third Logos, when fertilizing the chaotic matter contained in the semen and in the dorsal spine, fertilizing the Divine Mother, the Akashic principle, so that the inner universe, the solar bodies, are born. Thereafter, the Second Logos is born within those superior existential bodies of the Being, in order to work in the Great Work of the Father.

That which is above is like that which is below. That which is below is like that which is above. The cosmic events that are developed in a solar system are repeated in the atom. The great events that occur one after the other in the genesis of any galaxy are also repeated in the human microcosmos.

It is necessary to work first with the fire, and thereafter with the light. It is indispensable to work first with the Third Logos, in the ninth sphere, and then with the Second Logos.

The five elementary Initiations of Major Mysteries relate to the microcosmic cosmogenesis. The fire fertilizes the chaotic matter of the Divine Mother so that our solar bodies are born. Later, the best comes, the intervention of the Second Logos, the Venustic Initiation, having previously sacrificed oneself on behalf of humanity.

It is indispensable to know, it is urgent to comprehend, that the Venustic Initiation has seven esoteric degrees.

First: Birth in the manger of the world. The Inner Christ, filled with love for humanity, is always born in that inner manger that we carry within ourselves, that is unfortunately inhabited by the animal of passions, by the pluralized "I."

Second: Baptism of the initiate in the ethereal world, Christification of the vital body.

Third: Transfiguration of the Lord. The inner Christ shines in the head and sidereal face of the astral body of the initiate, as he shone in the face of Moses on Mount Nebo.

Fourth: Entrance into Jerusalem amidst palms and festivities. Christification of the mental body of the initiate.

Fifth: Veronica's sacred cloth, upon which the face of the master is engraved. Christification of the human soul or body of the conscious will.

Sixth: Christification of the spiritual soul (Buddhi). Formidable cosmic events in the Buddhic consciousness that unfortunately were not written in the four gospels; events of the cosmic drama intimately related to certain events of other planets of the solar system.

Seventh: The master is crucified and delivers the spirit to the Father, amidst lightning, thunder, and earthquakes. The woman always seals the sepulcher with a great stone, the Philosopher's Stone that symbolizes sex (the fight against Satan was terrible).

In a rigorous synthesis, these are the seven degrees of the Venustic Initiation. Enormous volumes can be written about each of these seven degrees.

The Christ, our Lord, will always be born within the humble individual stable of any prepared initiate.

The mother of the Lord has been, is, and always will be the Divine Mother Kundalini, the igneous serpent of our magical powers.

The kings of intelligence, the three wise kings, the three king-magicians, the true genii, will always recognize the Lord, so they will come to worship him.

The child will find himself always within great danger. Herod—the world, the tenebrous—will always want to slaughter him.

The baptism in the river Jordan of existence will always be indispensable, since the waters of life clean, transform, and baptize.

The transfiguration occurs when he interprets the law of Moses with total intelligence, by teaching the people and unfolding in his works all of the marvelous zeal of Elias.

The Lord will always come towards us walking upon the boisterous waves of the sea of life.

The intimate Lord will always establish an order in our mind, and he will give back the lost light to our eyes.

The inner Lord will always multiply the bread of the Eucharist for the nourishment and strength of our souls.

The Beloved incarnated within the initiate will preach along the roads of this great Jerusalem of the world, by delivering the message of the new era to humanity, and his face crowned with thorns—time and time again—will be forever engraved on the cloth of Veronica.

Formidable cosmic events will always be in the consciousness of the initiate, and among lightning, thunder, and great earthquakes of the soul, the Lord will always deliver his spirit to the Father by exclaiming, "My Father, into Thy hands I commend my spirit." Thereafter, the body placed in the sepulcher will repeat the resurrection after three days and a half.

This solar myth has two aspects: first, it represents the cosmic activity of the Second Logos, in the dawn of any new world arising from the womb of the Great Mother. The second aspect summarizes the life of any sacred individual that becomes an incarnation of the Second Logos, the Cosmic Christ.

In all times, the hero of the solar myth has been always presented as a human-god whose life unfolds and develops in accordance with the journey of the Sun, which is the cosmic vehicle of the Solar Logos.

In the past, in ancient times, the birth of Mithras was always celebrated in the winter solstice with great rejoicings.

In the ancient Egypt of the Pharaohs, Horus, divine spirit, son of Isis and Osiris, was also born in the winter solstice.

Nobody knows with exactitude the exact date of the birth of Jesus of Nazareth. There were 136 different dates assigned to the birth of Jesus. Thus, Gnostic initiates resolved with great wisdom to determine the date of the birth of Jesus as December 24th at midnight—that is to say, to the first minutes of the 25th of the same month.

In another solar myth, the divine savior, the inner Christ of any sacred individual, is always born from the womb of an immaculate virgin, the Divine Mother Kundalini. This reminds us of the Sun Child of December the 24th or 25th, advancing, being born, walking towards the north in the moments in which the constellation of Virgo, the immaculate virgin, shines, and is resplendent in the zenith. Whether in the cosmos or in the human being, the Sun, the Cosmic Christ, is always born from the womb of the virgin Cosmic Mother.

According to the cosmic drama wisely comprehended by Chinese initiates, Buddha is born from a virgin named Maya Devi.

The death and resurrection of the Lord in the equinox of spring are widely known, as well as his birth in the winter solstice.

On that date, Osiris died by the hands of Typhon, and was represented with his arms extended as if he was crucified.

In Babylon and Syria at that time, Tammuz's death was mourned every year. During that period of the spring equinox, many sacred mournings took place.

Adonis was mourned not only in Syria, but also in Greece.

In Persia, the death of Mithras was celebrated during the same period of the spring equinox.

The entire solar journey from its birth to its death and resurrection was represented in a dramatic manner in all schools of mysteries. The initiate constituted his life with the solar drama, through the Venustic Initiation becoming in fact a solar individual, a true human being.

The highest degree that a woman can reach is the degree of Celestial Virgin, which corresponds to the state of a living maitreya buddha.[98]

When a Celestial Virgin wants to reach the Venustic Initiation, she must renounce Nirvana and reincarnate in a new body.[99] In these times, in the valley of the Nile, in Egypt, the great being who was named Mary, the mother of Jesus of

---

98 Like the word Buddha, the word maitreya is a title, not a personal name. Anyone who enters the path of the bodhisattva and fully develops bodhichitta becomes a maitreya buddha, which literally means "one who is awakened in compassion." Not all buddhas follow the bodhisattva path (the direct path); most buddhas are buddhas pratyekas (nirvanis of the spiral path). As in esoteric Christianity we call Christ anyone who incarnates the Cosmic Christ and thereby becomes an expression of that force, likewise, in esoteric Buddhism we call Maitreya any buddha who renounces Nirvana for the sake of those who are suffering in ignorance.

99 The author expanded on this later: "...the woman can also go through, with complete clarity, all the five initiations of fire. When the woman (and this is something that I am going to fully clarify), if her body is too worn out, heavy, old, when she can no longer carry out the great work and needs to enter the Venustic initiations, then she is given a new body more favorable for her work, a body of masculine order. Already with that vehicle, loaded with virility, she can, in fact, get into the work of the Venustic initiations; that is all. But if the woman is still strong, young, if she has truly managed to reach the heights of adepthood in a single reincarnation, she, too, can enter Venustic initiations with that feminine body. She would not be forced, in this case, to change vehicles, with the same one she has she could enter the Venustic initiations. This is not contradictory to what I am saying. What happens is that many ladies reach the fifth initiation of fire when they are already very old, when they already have to disincarnate. So the great law gives them a masculine vehicle to continue their work. The case of Blavatsky is a concrete fact: she disincarnated when she was very old. So, she will now be given a male body so that she can enter the Venustic initiations with energy. But I repeat: if the body is young, if the body can withstand the ordeals of initiation, if it can still transmute its creative energies, well, it can also achieve the Venustic initiations in its present existence and with the body she has; that is all." –The End Times Have Arrived

Nazareth, is incarnated in a male body. Likewise H.P.B., the wise theosophical author who wrote the six volumes of *The Secret Doctrine,* wants to attain the Venustic Initiation, thus she is being prepared in order to reincarnate in a male body. What we are stating does not have to dishearten the Nirvanis.

The married woman and man who work in the flaming forge of Vulcan, the married woman and man who work in the ninth sphere, can create their solar bodies and become respectively a Virgin of Nirvana and a living Buddha, with powers over the fire, the air, the water, and the earth. However, the Venustic Initiation is another thing. This is only for true human beings. Thus, any Virgin of Nirvana, any living Buddha, can reincarnate in a new body and reach the Venustic Initiation.

Whenever the Solar Logos needs to come into the world to initiate a new era, it is incarnated in a human being duly prepared for the Venustic Initiation.

There are twelve saviors; this means twelve avatars that correspond to the twelve signs of the zodiac. The mission of each avatar is to initiate the time of activity corresponding to the sign that humanity is going to enter. Aries, Taurus, etc., had their corresponding avatars. There are twelve saviors through whom the living Christ expresses himself. The incarnation of the Solar Logos in the manger of the world is a formidable cosmic event.

Thus, as in any world that is arising, where the incarnated Christ must break through the terrible vortex of the wild jungle, surrounded by all types of dangers, likewise the Golden Child of sexual alchemy, the inner Christ born within any sacred individual, must break through, must grow up and develop amidst the animals of the manger, amidst the animals of desire, surrounded by all types of dangers and adversities.

Unfortunately, in the beginning, the initiate has not yet dissolved the "I." The animals of his inner stable are alive. The initiate has not reached perfection yet, even though he is a Buddha. Thus, the child must grow and develop amidst all these adversities.

In the worlds that are arising to existence, the Christ is developed, crucified, dies, and resurrected within the entrails of all of that which is created, so that all beings can have life, and have it in abundance.

In the initiate who reaches the Venustic Initiation, the Christ must be born, grow, die, and resurrect in order to work with extreme intensity in the great work of the Father.

The sacred scriptures state:

> *"It came to pass, when Jesus had risen from the dead that he passed eleven years discoursing with his disciples, and instructing them... about the four and twentieth mystery (from where the twelve saviors of the world are born)."* –Samael Aun Weor, The Gnostic Bible, The Pistis Sophia Unveiled

Final Salutations

Beloved,

We have stated in this 1966-1967 Christmas Message all we had to say. You must study it intensively. It is not enough to read this message once, like when one reads a newspaper. This message is for study throughout our life, and for deep comprehension in all of the levels of our mind.

You must not be like fluttering butterflies that today are in one school and tomorrow in another, that waste their time miserably, reading and theorizing, but without performing absolutely anything.

Do not be like the profaners of mysteries who today study the doctrine and tomorrow mock it.

Study and work. This message is for the realization of your own inner Self.

Remember that we are delivering to you the second part of the Gnostic teachings. All the summum of our esoteric Christic doctrine will be condensed within the Christmas Message of each year.

In former times, the message was a simple pamphlet. Now this message will be a book that you will receive every year at Christmas.

It is necessary for the Gnostic Lumisials to become meditation halls. It is urgent to practice meditation in groups, in accordance with the lesson of chapter eighteen of this 1966-1967 Christmas Message.

Remember beloved, in the narration about the Chinese Master Wu Wen we taught a practical technique for meditation.

It is necessary to study this Christmas Message in all Lumisials. Thus, converse about it, teach it, analyze it, and comprehend it.

Beloved, I wish for you a Merry Christmas and prosperous New Year 1967. May the Star of Bethlehem shine on your path. Let peace be in your hearts. Let joy be in your homes.

Inverential peace.

Glossary

Absolute: Abstract space; that which is without attributes or limitations. Also known as sunyata, void, emptiness, Parabrahman, Adi-buddha, and many other names.

"The Absolute is the Being of all Beings. The Absolute is that which Is, which always has Been, and which always will Be. The Absolute is expressed as Absolute Abstract Movement and Repose. The Absolute is the cause of Spirit and of Matter, but It is neither Spirit nor Matter. The Absolute is beyond the mind; the mind cannot understand It. Therefore, we have to intuitively understand Its nature." –Samael Aun Weor, *Tarot and Kabbalah*

"In the Absolute we go beyond karma and the gods, beyond the law. The mind and the individual consciousness are only good for mortifying our lives. In the Absolute we do not have an individual mind or individual consciousness; there, we are the unconditioned, free and absolutely happy Being. The Absolute is life free in its movement, without conditions, limitless, without the mortifying fear of the law, life beyond spirit and matter, beyond karma and suffering, beyond thought, word and action, beyond silence and sound, beyond forms." –Samael Aun Weor, *The Major Mysteries*

Alchemy: Al (as a connotation of the Arabic word Allah: al-, the + ilah, God) means "The God." Also Al (Hebrew) for "highest" or El "God." Chem or Khem is from kimia (Greek) which means "to fuse or cast a metal." Also from Khem, the ancient name of Egypt. The synthesis is Al-Kimia: "to fuse with the highest" or "to fuse with God."

Aquarius: An era of time under the influence of the zodiacal sign of Aquarius that will last for approximately 2,140 years. The new Aquarian era began with the celestial conjunction of February 4-5, 1962. On February 4-5, 1962, exactly when there was a new moon AND a full solar eclipse, there was also an extraordinary celestial conjunction of the seven primary planets with the Earth. The Sun, the Moon, Mercury, Venus, Mars, Jupiter, and Saturn were all visibly grouped close together, and their orbits were aligned with the Earth. This event signaled a change of era, similar to how the hands of a clock move into a new day. The Earth had completed an era of approximately 2,140 years under the influence of Pisces, and then entered an era influenced by Aquarius.

When the age of Aquarius arrived, humanity entered into a very new situation. With the new celestial influence we saw the arrival of a huge shift in society: mass rebellion against the old ways, sexual experimentation, giant social earthquakes shaking up all the old traditions. We also saw the arrival in the West of a strong spiritual longing, and deep thirst for true, authentic spiritual experience. These two elements: 1) rebellion to tradition and 2) thirst for spiritual knowledge are a direct effect of the influence of Aquarius, the most revolutionary sign of the zodiac. Aquarius is the Water Carrier, whose occult significance is knowledge, the bringer of knowledge. With the new age came a sudden revealing of all the hidden knowledge. The doors to the mysteries were thrown open so that humanity can save itself from itself. Of course, the Black Lodge, ever-eager to mislead humanity, has produced so much false spirituality and so many false schools that it is very difficult to find the real and genuine path.

"The majority of the tenebrous brothers and sisters of Aquarius are wicked people who are going around teaching black magic." —Samael Aun Weor, *The Major Mysteries*

"The age of sex, the new Aquarian Age, is at hand. The sexual glands are controlled by the planet Uranus which is the ruling planet of the constellation of Aquarius. Thus, sexual alchemy is in fact the science of the new Aquarian Age. Sexual Magic will be officially accepted in the universities of the new Aquarian Age. Those who presume to be messengers of the new Aquarian Age, but nevertheless hate the Arcanum A.Z.F., provide more than enough evidence that they are truly impostors, this is because the new Aquarian Age is governed by the regent of sex. This regent is the planet Uranus. Sexual energy is the finest energy of the infinite cosmos. Sexual energy can convert us into angels or demons. The image of truth is found deposited in sexual energy. The cosmic design of Adam Christ is found deposited in sexual energy." —Samael Aun Weor, *The Perfect Matrimony*

To learn more about the Aquarian era, read *Christ and the Virgin* by Samael Aun Weor.

Arcanum: (Latin. plural: arcana). A secret, a mystery. The root of the term "ark" as in the Ark of Noah and the Ark of the Covenent.

Arcanum A.Z.F.: The practice of sexual transmutation as couple (male-female), a technique known in Tantra and Alchemy. Arcanum refers to a hidden truth or law. A.Z.F. stands for A (agua, water), Z (azufre, sulfur), F (fuego, fire), and is thus: water + fire = consciousness. . Also, A (azoth = chemical element that refers to fire). A & Z are the first and last letters of the alphabet thus referring to the Alpha & Omega (beginning & end).

Aryan Race: "(Sanskrit) arya [from the verbal root to rise, tend upward] Holy, hallowed, highly evolved or especially trained; a title of the Hindu rishis [initiates]. Originally a term of ethical as well as intellectual and spiritual excellence, belonging to those who had completely mastered the aryasatyani (holy truths) and who had entered upon the aryamarga (path leading to moksha or nirvana). It was originally applicable only to the initiates or adepts of the ancient Aryan peoples, but today Aryan has become the name of a race of the human family in its various branches. All ancient peoples had their own term for initiates or adepts, as for instance among the ancient Hebrews the generic name Israel, or Sons of Israel." —Theosophical Glossary

"From Sanskrit [=a]rya excellent, honorable; akin to the name of the country Iran, and perh. to Erin, Ireland, and the early name of this people, at least in Asia. 1. One of a primitive people supposed to have lived in prehistoric times, in Central Asia, east of the Caspian Sea, and north of the Hindoo Koosh and Paropamisan Mountains, and to have been the stock from which sprang the Hindoo, Persian, Greek, Latin, Celtic, Teutonic, Slavonic, and other races; one of that ethnological division of mankind called also Indo-European or Indo-Germanic." —Webster's Revised Unabridged Dictionary

While formerly it was believed that the ancient Aryans were European (white), most scientists now believe that the ancient people commonly referred to as Aryan were the original inhabitants of India, which Manu called Aryavarta, "Abode of the Aryans." However, in universal Gnosticism, the word Aryan refers not to "white people" or to an ancient, dead civilization, but instead refers to to the vast majority of the population of this planet. In Gnosis, all modern races are "Aryan."

Astral: This term is derived from "pertaining to or proceeding from the stars," but in the esoteric knowledge it refers to the emotional aspect of the fifth dimension, which in Hebrew is called Hod.

Astral Body: What is commonly called the astral body is not the true astral body, it is rather the lunar protoplasmatic body, also known as the kama rupa (Sanskrit, "body of desires") or "dream body" (Tibetan rmi-lam-gyi lus). The true astral body is solar (being superior to lunar nature) and must be created, as the Master Jesus indicated in the Gospel of John 3:5-6, "Except a man be born of water and of the Spirit, he cannot enter into the kingdom of God. That which is born of the flesh is flesh; and that which is born of the Spirit is spirit." The solar astral body is created as a result of the Third Initiation of Major Mysteries (Serpents of Fire), and is perfected in the Third Serpent of Light. In Tibetan Buddhism, the solar astral body is known as the illusory body (sgyu-lus). This body is related to the emotional center and to the sephirah Hod.

"Really, only those who have worked with the Maithuna (White Tantra) for many years can possess the astral body." —Samael Aun Weor, *The Elimination of Satan's Tail*

Atom: While modern science studies atoms as the basic unit of matter, they are ignoring the two other essential aspects of each atom: energy and consciousness.

"Every atom is a trio of matter, energy and consciousness. The consciousness of every atom is always an intelligent elemental. If the materialists are not capable of seeing those elementals, it is because they still do not know the scientific procedures that allow us to see them. We have special methods in order to see those creatures. Indeed, the atom is a truly infinitely small planetary system. Those planetary systems of the atoms are formed by ultra-atomic ternaries that spin around their centers of gravitation. The atom with its Alpha, Beta, and Gamma rays is a trio of matter, energy and consciousness." –Samael Aun Weor, *Sexology, the Basis of Endocrinology and Criminology*

Thus understood as being more than mere matter, atoms have great significance for all living creatures, since atoms form the basis for all living things. That is why the spiritual classic *The Dayspring of Youth* by M explains that atoms are "Minute bodies of intelligence possessing the dual attributes of Nature and man." While there are many types and levels of such atomic intelligences, both positive and negative, some of particular importance are Aspiring atoms, Destructive atoms, the Nous atom, Informer atoms, Scholar atoms, etc.

"Life will not be fully understood until we recognise the living forces within us and transplant atoms of a higher nature into the body. This will eventually help humanity to become the personification of justice. Our atomic centres are similar to the starry clusters in the sky, and each atom is a minute intelligence revolving within its own atmosphere. When we aspire we unite ourselves to atoms that have preceded us in evolution; for they evolve as we evolve: this body being their university, and they prepare the path for us to follow." –*The Dayspring of Youth* by M

"The atom of the Father is situated in the root of the nose; this is the atom of willpower. The seven serpents ascend by means of willpower, by dominating the animal impulse. The atom of the Father is situated in the root of the nose; this is the atom of willpower. The seven serpents ascend by means of willpower, by dominating the animal impulse. The atom of the Son is in the pituitary gland, whose exponent is the Nous atom (the Son of Man) in the heart. The angelic atom of the Holy Spirit shines in the pineal gland, within the chakra Sahasrara. The atom of the Father governs or controls the right ganglionary chord Pingala within which the solar atoms, the positive force, ascends. The atom of the Son governs the Sushumna canal, within which the neutral forces ascend. The atom of the Holy Spirit governs the Ida canal, within which the negative forces ascend. This is why it is related with our creative sexual forces and with the rays of the moon, which are intimately related with the reproduction of the races. Each of the seven chakras from the spinal medulla is governed by an angelic atom." –Samael Aun Weor, *Kabbalah of the Mayan Mysteries*

Bodhisattva: (Sanskrit) Literally, the Sanskrit term bodhi means "enlightened, wisdom, perfect knowledge," while sattva means "essence, goodness." Therefore, the term bodhisattva literally means "essence of wisdom."

A bodhisattva is a human soul (consciousness) who is on the direct path. A bodhisattva is the messenger or servant of their inner Being / Buddha. The inner Being or Buddha resides in the superior worlds, and sends the bodhisattva into the lower worlds to work for others.

"The bodhisattva is the human soul of a master. The master is the internal God [Atman, the Innermost Buddha]." –Samael Aun Weor, *The Aquarian Message*

One becomes a bodhisattva upon:

- creating the solar bodies (astral, mental, causal) through sexual transmutation
- choosing to enter the direct path to the absolute rather than the slower spiral path
- having developed sufficient Bodhichitta (love for others in combination with comprehension of the absolute)

The word bodhisattva is a title or honorific that describes a level of consciousness earned through internal initiation, not physical. A bodhisattva is a person who through dedication to compassionate service to humanity has some degree of Bodhichitta – a psychological quality uniting deep compassion with profound insight into the nature of reality, the Absolute – and has also created the solar bodies, which correspond to the first five serpents of kundalini (candali).

In Tibetan Buddhism the term bodhisattva is sometimes publicly used in a more "generous" way to include those who aspire to become bodhisattvas.

The Tibetan translation of bodhisattva is jangchub sempa. Jangchub (Sanskrit bodhi) means "enlightenment," and sempa (Sanskrit sattva) means "hero" or a being, therefore meaning "enlightened hero." The word jangchub is from jang, "the overcoming and elimination of all obstructive forces," and chub, "realization of full knowledge." Sempa is a reference to great compassion.

"...bodhisattvas are beings who, out of intense compassion, never shift their attention away from sentient beings; they are perpetually concerned for the welfare of all beings, and they dedicate themselves entirely to securing that welfare. Thus the very name bodhisattva indicates a being who, through wisdom, heroically focuses on the attainment of enlightenment out of compassionate concern for all beings. The word itself conveys the key qualities of such an infinitely altruistic being." —The 14th Dalai Lama

"We, the bodhisattvas of compassion who love humanity immensely, state: as long as there is a single tear in any human eye, as long as there is even one suffering heart, we refuse to accept the happiness of Nirvana... We must seek the means to become more and more useful to this wretched, suffering humanity." —Samael Aun Weor, *The Major Mysteries*

Strictly speaking, the term bodhisattva addresses not a physical person but the human soul of someone walking the Direct Path. The bodhisttva is the human soul (Tipereth, the causal body), which is the servant or messenger of the inner Being (Chesed). The human soul earns the title bodhisattva by —because of love for humanity – choosing to advance spiritually by entering the terrifying Direct Path instead of the easier Spiral Path, a choice that is made only after finishing the Fifth Initiation of Fire (Tiphereth, causal body). By means of this sacrifice, this individual incarnates the Christ (Chenresig, Kuan Yin, Avalokitesvara), thereby embodying the supreme source of wisdom and compassion. That human soul is then a mixture of the divine and human, and by carrying that light within becomes a messenger or active exponent of the light. The Direct Path demands rapid and complete liberation from the ego, a route that only very few take, due to the fact that one must pay the entirety of one's karma imminently. Those who have taken this road have been the most remarkable figures in human history: Jesus, Buddha, Mohamed, Krishna, Moses, Padmasambhava, Milarepa, Joan of Arc, Fu-Xi, and many others whose names are not remembered or known.

Even among bodhisattvas there are many levels of Being: to be a bodhisattva does not mean that one is enlightened. In fact, there are many fallen bodhisattvas: human souls who resumed poor behavior and are thus cut off from their inner Being.

"Let no one seek his own good, but the good of his neighbor." —1 Corinthians 10.24

"The truly humble Bodhisattva never praises himself. The humble Bodhisattva says, 'I am just a miserable slug from the mud of the earth, I am a nobody. My person has no value. The work is what is worthy.' The Bodhisattva is the human soul of a Master. The Master is the internal God." —Samael Aun Weor, *The Aquarian Message*

"Let it be understood that a Bodhisattva is a seed, a germ, with the possibility of transcendental, divine development by means of pressure coming from the Height." —Samael Aun Weor, *The Gnostic Bible: The Pistis Sophia Unveiled*

Interestingly, the Christ in Hebrew is called Chokmah, which means "wisdom," and in Sanskrit the same is Vishnu, the root of the word "wisdom." It is Vishnu who sent his Avatars into the world in order to aid humanity. These avatars were Krishna, Buddha, Rama, and the Avatar of this age: the Avatar Kalki.

Centers, Seven: The human being has seven centers of psychological activity. The first five are the Intellectual, Emotional, Motor, Instinctive, and Sexual Centers. However, through inner development one learns how to utilize the Superior Emotional and Superior Intellectual Centers. Most people do not use these two at all.

Chakra: (Sanskrit) Literally, "wheel." The chakras are subtle centers of energetic transformation. There are hundreds of chakras in our hidden physiology, but seven primary ones related to the awakening of consciousness.

"The Chakras are centres of Shakti as vital force... The Chakras are not perceptible to the gross senses. Even if they were perceptible in the living body which they help to organise, they disappear with the disintegration of organism at death." —Swami Sivananda, *Kundalini Yoga*

"The chakras are points of connection through which the divine energy circulates from one to another vehicle of the human being." —Samael Aun Weor, *Aztec Christic Magic*

Chaos: (Greek ⊠⊠⊠⊠) khaos "abyss, that which gapes wide open, is vast and empty." There are three primary applications of this term.

"The first Chaos from which the cosmos emerged is between the Sephiroth Binah and Chesed. The second Chaos, from where the fundamental principles of the human being emerged, exists within Yesod-Mercury, which is the sexual human center. The third Chaos, the Infernal Worlds, exists below the Thirteenth Aeons in the region of Klipoth, in the underworld." - Samael Aun Weor, *The Pistis Sophia Unveiled*

Primarily, chaos is the primitive state of the universe, from which occurs creation (Genesis). The abyss (not the inferior abyss), or the "Great Deep." Personified as the Egyptian Goddess Neith, the Great Mother, the Immaculate Virgin from which arises all matter. The Chaos is WITHIN the Ain Soph. The primitive state of the universe. Esoterically, a reference to the semen, both in the microcosm and the macrocosm. Alchemically, it is said to be a mixture of water & fire, and it holds the seeds of the cosmos.

"In truth Chaos came into being the very first." - Hesiod, *Theogony*

"First I sung the obscurity of ancient Chaos, How the Elements were ordered, and the Heaven reduced to bound; And the generation of the wide-bosomed Earth, and the depth of the Sea, And Eros the most ancient, self-perfecting, and of manifold design; How he generated all things, and parted them from one another." - Orphic fragment (Greek)

Chastity: Although modern usage has rendered the term chastity virtually meaningless to most people, its original meaning and usage clearly indicate "moral purity" upon the basis of "sexual purity." Contemporary usage implies "repression" or "abstinence," which have nothing to do with real chastity. True chastity is a rejection of impure sexuality. True chastity is pure sexuality, or the activity of sex in harmony with our true nature, as explained in the secret doctrine. Properly used, the word chastity refers to sexual fidelity or honor.

"The generative energy, which, when we are loose, dissipates and makes us unclean, when we are continent invigorates and inspires us. Chastity is the flowering of man; and what are called Genius, Heroism, Holiness, and the like, are but various fruits which succeed it." —Henry David Thoreau, *Walden*

Christ: Derived from the Greek Christos, "the Anointed One," and Krestos, whose esoteric meaning is "fire." The word Christ is a title, not a personal name.

"Indeed, Christ is a Sephirothic Crown (Kether, Chokmah and Binah) of incommensurable wisdom, whose purest atoms shine within Chokmah, the world of the Ophanim. Christ is not the Monad, Christ is not the Theosophical Septenary; Christ is not the Jivan-Atman. Christ is the Central Sun. Christ is the ray that unites us to the Absolute." —Samael Aun Weor, *Tarot and Kabbalah*

"The Gnostic Church adores the saviour of the world, Jesus. The Gnostic Church knows that Jesus incarnated Christ, and that is why they adore him. Christ is not a human nor a divine individual. Christ is a title given to all fully self-realized masters. Christ is the Army of the Voice. Christ is the Verb. The Verb is far beyond the body, the soul and the Spirit. Everyone who is able to incarnate the Verb receives in fact the title of Christ. Christ is the Verb itself. It is necessary for everyone of us to incarnate the Verb (Word). When the Verb becomes flesh in us we speak with the verb of light. In actuality, several masters have incarnated the Christ. In secret India, the Christ Yogi Babaji has lived for millions of years; Babaji is immortal. The great master of wisdom Kout Humi also incarnated the Christ. Sanat Kumara, the founder of the great College of Initiates of the White Lodge, is another living Christ. In the past, many incarnated the Christ. In the present, some have incarnated the Christ. In the future many will incarnate the Christ. John the Baptist also incarnated the Christ. John the Baptist is a living Christ. The difference between Jesus and the other masters that also incarnated the Christ has to do with hierarchy. Jesus is the highest Solar initiate of the cosmos..." –Samael Aun Weor, *The Perfect Matrimony*

Consciousness: The modern English term consciousness is derived primarily from the Latin word conscius, "knowing, aware." Thus, consciousness is the basic factor of perception and understanding, and is therefore the basis of any living thing. Since living things are not equal and have a great deal of variety, so too does consciousness: it has infinite potential for development, either towards the heights of perfection or towards the depths of degeneration.

"Wherever there is life, there is consciousness. Consciousness is inherent to life as humidity is inherent to water." –Samael Aun Weor, *Sexology, the Basis of Endocrinology and Criminology*

"It is vital to understand and develop the conviction that consciousness has the potential to increase to an infinite degree." –The 14th Dalai Lama

"Light and consciousness are two phenomena of the same thing; to a lesser degree of consciousness, corresponds a lesser degree of light; to a greater degree of consciousness, a greater degree of light." –Samael Aun Weor, *The Esoteric Treatise of Hermetic Astrology*

Devolution: (Latin) From devolvere: backwards evolution, degeneration. The natural mechanical inclination for all matter and energy in nature to return towards their state of inert uniformity. Related to the Arcanum Ten: Retribution, the Wheel of Samsara. Devolution is the inverse process of evolution. As evolution is the complication of matter or energy, devolution is the slow process of nature to simplify matter or energy by applying forces to it. Through devolution, protoplasmic matter and energy descend, degrade, and increase in density within the infradimensions of nature to finally reach the center of the earth where they attain their ultimate state of inert uniformity. Devolution transfers the psyche, moral values, consciousness, or psychological responsibilities to inferior degradable organisms (Klipoth) through the surrendering of our psychological values to animal behaviors, especially sexual degeneration.

Divine Mother: The Divine Mother is the eternal, feminine principle, which is formless, and further unfolds into many levels, aspects, and manifestations.

"Devi or Sakti is the Mother of Nature. She is Nature Itself. The whole world is Her body. Mountains are Her bones. Rivers are Her veins. Ocean is Her bladder. Sun, moon are Her eyes. Wind is Her breath. Agni is Her mouth. She runs this world show. Sakti is symbolically female; but It is, in reality, neither male nor female. It is only a Force which manifests Itself in various forms. The five elements and their combinations are the external manifestations of the Mother. Intelligence, discrimination, psychic power, and will are Her internal manifestations." —Swami Sivananda

"Among the Aztecs, she was known as Tonantzin, among the Greeks as chaste Diana. In Egypt she was Isis, the Divine Mother, whose veil no mortal has lifted. There is no doubt at all that esoteric Christianity has never forsaken the worship of the Divine Mother Kundalini. Obviously she is Marah, or better said, RAM-IO, MARY. What orthodox religions did not specify, at least with regard to the exoteric or public circle, is the aspect of Isis in her individual human form. Clearly, it was taught only in secret to the Initiates that this Divine Mother exists individually within each human being. It cannot be emphasized enough that Mother-God, Rhea, Cybele, Adonia, or whatever we wish to call her, is a variant of our own individual Being in the here and now. Stated explicitly, each of us has our own particular, individual Divine Mother." —Samael Aun Weor, *The Great Rebellion*

"Devi Kundalini, the Consecrated Queen of Shiva, our personal Divine Cosmic Individual Mother, assumes five transcendental mystic aspects in every creature, which we must enumerate:

1. The unmanifested Prakriti

2. The chaste Diana, Isis, Tonantzin, Maria or better said Ram-Io

3. The terrible Hecate, Persephone, Coatlicue, queen of the infemos and death; terror of love and law

4. The special individual Mother Nature, creator and architect of our physical organism

5. The Elemental Enchantress to whom we owe every vital impulse, every instinct." —Samael Aun Weor, *The Secret of the Golden Flower*

Ego: The multiplicity of contradictory psychological elements that we have inside are in their sum the "ego." Each one is also called "an ego" or an "I." Every ego is a psychological defect which produces suffering. The ego is three (related to our Three Brains or three centers of psychological processing), seven (capital sins), and legion (in their infinite variations).

"The ego is the root of ignorance and pain." –Samael Aun Weor, *The Esoteric Treatise of Hermetic Astrology*

"The Being and the ego are incompatible. The Being and the ego are like water and oil. They can never be mixed... The annihilation of the psychic aggregates (egos) can be made possible only by radically comprehending our errors through meditation and by the evident Self-reflection of the Being." –Samael Aun Weor, *The Pistis Sophia Unveiled*

Elohim: [אלהים] An Hebrew term with a wide variety of meanings. In Christian translations of scripture, it is one of many words translated to the generic word "God," but whose actual meaning depends upon the context. For example:

1. In Kabbalah, אלהים is a name of God the relates to many levels of the Tree of Life. In the world of Atziluth, the word is related to divnities of the sephiroth Binah (Jehovah Elohim, mentioned especially in Genesis), Geburah, and Hod. In the world of Briah, it is related beings of Netzach and Hod.

2. El [אל] is "god," Eloah [אלה] is "goddess," therefore the plural Elohim refers to "gods and goddesses," and is commonly used to refer to Cosmocreators or Dhyan-Choans.

3. אלה Elah or Eloah is "goddess." Yam [ים] is "sea" or "ocean." Therefore אלהים Elohim can be אלה-ים "the sea goddess" [i.e. Aphrodite, Stella Maris, etc.]

There are many more meanings of "Elohim." In general, Elohim refers to high aspects of divinity.

"Each one of us has his own Interior Elohim. The Interior Elohim is the Being of our Being. The Interior Elohim is our Father-Mother. The Interior Elohim is the ray that emanates from Aelohim." –Samael Aun Weor, *The Gnostic Bible: The Pistis Sophia Unveiled*

Essence: From Chinese 體 ti, which literally means "substance, body" and is often translated as "essence," to indicate that which is always there throughout transformations. In gnosis, the term essence refers to our consciousness, which remains fundamentally the same, in spite of the many transformations it suffers, especially life, death, and being trapped in psychological defects. A common example given in Buddhism is a glass of water: even if filled with dirt and impurities, the water is still there; its original pure essence is latent and ultimately unchanged by the presence of filth. However, one would not want to drink it that way. Just so with the Essence (the consciousness): our Essence is trapped in impurities; to use it properly, it must be cleaned first.

"Singularly radiating is the wondrous Light;
Free is it from the bondage of matter and the senses.
Not binding by words and letters.
The Essence [體] is nakedly exposed in its pure eternity.
Never defiled is the Mind-nature;
It exists in perfection from the very beginning.

By merely casting away your delusions
The Suchness of Buddhahood is realized." –Shen Tsan

"Zen, however, is interested not in these different "fields" but only in penetrating to 體 the Essence, or the innermost core of the mind for it holds that once this core is grasped, all else will become relatively insignificant, and crystal clear... only by transcending [attachment] may one come to the innermost core of Mind–the perfectly free and thoroughly nonsubstantial illuminating-Voidness. This illuminating-Void character, empty yet dynamic, is the Essence (Chinese: 體 ti) of the mind... The Essence of mind is the Illuminating-Void Suchness." –G.C.Chang, The Practice of Zen (1959)

"Without question the Essence, or consciousness, which is the same thing, sleeps deeply... The Essence in itself is very beautiful. It came from above, from the stars. Lamentably, it is smothered deep within all these "I's" we carry inside. By contrast, the Essence can retrace its steps, return to the point of origin, go back to the stars, but first it must liberate itself from its evil companions, who have trapped it within the slums of perdition. Human beings have three percent free Essence, and the other ninety-seven percent is imprisoned within the "I's"." –Samael Aun Weor, *The Great Rebellion*

"A percentage of psychic Essence is liberated when a defect is disintegrated. Thus, the psychic Essence which is bottled up within our defects will be completely liberated when we disintegrate each and every one of our false values, in other words, our defects. Thus, the radical transformation of ourselves will occur when the totality of our Essence is liberated. Then, in that precise moment, the eternal values of the Being will express themselves through us. Unquestionably, this would be marvelous not only for us, but also for all of humanity." –Samael Aun Weor, *The Revolution of the Dialectic*

Evolution: "It is not possible for the true human being (the Self-realized Being) to appear through the mechanics of evolution. We know very well that evolution and its twin sister devolution are nothing else but two laws which constitute the mechanical axis of all Nature. One evolves to a certain perfectly defined point, and then the devolving process follows. Every ascent is followed by a descent and vice-versa." –Samael Aun Weor, *Treatise of Revolutionary Psychology.*

"Evolution is a process of complication of energy." –Samael Aun Weor, *The Perfect Matrimony*

Fohat: (Theosophical/Tibetan) A term used by H.P. Blavatsky to represent the active (male) potency of the Shakti (female sexual power) in nature, the essence of cosmic electricity, vital force. As explained in *The Secret Doctrine*, "He (Fohat) is, metaphysically, the objectivised thought of the gods; the "Word made flesh" on a lower scale, and the messenger of Cosmic and human ideations: the active force in Universal Life.... In India, Fohat is connected with Vishnu and Surya in the early character of the (first)

God; for Vishnu is not a high god in the Rig Veda. The name Vishnu is from the root vish, "to pervade," and Fohat is called the "Pervader" and the Manufacturer, because he shapes the atoms from crude material..." The term fohat has recently been linked with the Tibetan verb phro-wa and the noun spros-pa. These two terms are listed in Jäschke's Tibetan-English Dictionary (1881) as, for phro-wa, "to proceed, issue, emanate from, to spread, in most cases from rays of light..." while for spros-pa he gives "business, employment, activity."

Fornication: Originally, the term fornication was derived from the Indo-European word gwher, whose meanings relate to heat and burning. Fornication means to make the heat (solar fire) of the seed (sexual power) leave the body through voluntary orgasm. Any voluntary orgasm is fornication, whether between a married man and woman, or an unmarried man and woman, or through masturbation, or in any other case; this is explained by Moses: "A man from whom there is a discharge of semen, shall immerse all his flesh in water, and he shall remain unclean until evening. And any garment or any leather [object] which has semen on it, shall be immersed in water, and shall remain unclean until evening. A woman with whom a man cohabits, whereby there was [a discharge of] semen, they shall immerse in water, and they shall remain unclean until evening." —Leviticus 15:16-18

Primarily, to fornicate is to spill the sexual energy through the orgasm. Those who "deny themselves" restrain the sexual energy, and "walk in the midst of the fire" without being burned. Those who restrain the sexual energy, who renounce the orgasm, remember God in themselves, and do not defile themselves with animal passion, "for the temple of God is holy, which temple ye are."

"Whosoever is born of God doth not commit sin; for his seed remaineth in him: and he cannot sin, because he is born of God." —1 John 3:9

This is why neophytes always took a vow of sexual abstention, so that they could prepare themselves for marriage, in which they would have sexual relations but not release the sexual energy through the orgasm. This is why Paul advised:

"...they that have wives be as though they had none..." —I Corinthians 7:29

"A fornicator is an individual who has intensely accustomed his genital organs to copulate (with orgasm). Yet, if the same individual changes his custom of copulation to the custom of no copulation, then he transforms himself into a chaste person. We have as an example the astonishing case of Mary Magdalene, who was a famous prostitute. Mary Magdalene became the famous Saint Mary Magdalene, the repented prostitute. Mary Magdalene became the chaste disciple of Christ." —Samael Aun Weor, *The Revolution of Beelzebub*

Gnosis: (Greek) Knowledge.

1. The word Gnosis refers to the knowledge we acquire through our own experience, as opposed to knowledge that we are told or believe in. Gnosis - by whatever name in history or culture - is conscious, experiential knowledge, not merely intellectual or conceptual knowledge, belief, or theory. This term is synonymous with the Hebrew "daath" and the Sanskrit "jna."

2. The tradition that embodies the core wisdom or knowledge of humanity.

"Gnosis is the flame from which all religions sprouted, because in its depth Gnosis is religion. The word "religion" comes from the Latin word "religare," which implies "to link the Soul to God"; so Gnosis is the very pure flame from where all religions sprout, because Gnosis is knowledge, Gnosis is wisdom." –Samael Aun Weor from the lecture entitled *The Esoteric Path*

"The secret science of the Sufis and of the Whirling Dervishes is within Gnosis. The secret doctrine of Buddhism and of Taoism is within Gnosis. The sacred magic of the Nordics is within Gnosis. The wisdom of Hermes, Buddha, Confucius, Mohammed and Quetzalcoatl, etc., etc., is within Gnosis. Gnosis is the doctrine of Christ." –Samael Aun Weor, *The Revolution of Beelzebub*

Hasnamuss: Plural "hasnamussen." A term used by Gurdjieff in reference to a person with a divided consciousness: part of it is free and natural, and part is trapped in the ego. In synthesis, everyone who has ego is an hasnamuss. Although there are many variations and kinds of hasnamuss, there are four basic types:

- mortal: the common person
- those with the solar astral body
- those with the solar bodies created
- fallen angels

These are described in detail by Samael Aun Weor in his lecture "The Master Key."

"The Twice-born who does not reduce his lunar ego to cosmic dust converts himself into an abortion of the Cosmic Mother. He becomes a Marut, and there are thousands of types of Maruts. Certain oriental sects and some Muslim tribes commit the lamentable error of rendering cult to all of those families of Maruts. Every Marut, every hasnamuss has in fact two personalities: one white and another black (one solar and another lunar). The Innermost, the Being dressed with the solar electronic bodies, is the white personality of the hasnamuss, and the pluralized "I" dressed with theprotoplasmic lunar bodies is the hasnamuss' black personality. Therefore, these Maruts have a double center of gravity." –Samael Aun Weor

Gurdjieff described these qualities of the hasnamuss:

- Every kind of depravity, conscious as well as unconscious

- The feeling of self-satisfaction from leading others astray
- The irresistible inclination to destroy the existence of other breathing creatures
- The urge to become free from the necessity of actualizing the being-efforts demanded by Nature
- The attempt by every kind of artificiality to conceal from others what in their opinion are one's physical defects
- The calm self-contentment in the use of what is not personally deserved
- The striving to be not what one is.

Hydrogen: (From *hydro-* water, *gen-* generate, genes, genesis, etc.) The hydrogen is the simplest element on the periodic table and in Gnosticism it is recognized as the element that is the building block of all forms of matter. Hydrogen is a packet of solar light. The solar light (the light that comes from the sun) is the reflection of the Okidanok, the Cosmic Christ, which creates and sustains every world. This element is the fecundated water, generated water (hydro). The water is the source of all life. Everything that we eat, breathe and all of the impressions that we receive are in the form of various structures of hydrogen. Samael Aun Weor often will place a note (Do, Re, Mi...) and a number related with the vibration and atomic weight (level of complexity) with a particular hydrogen. For example, Samael Aun Weor constantly refers to the Hydrogen Si-12. "Si" is the highest note in the octave and it is the result of the notes that come before it. This particular hydrogen is always related to the forces of Yesod, which is the synthesis and coagulation of all food, air and impressions that we have previously received. Food begins at Do-768, air begins at Do-384, and impressions begin at Do-48.

Illuminating Void: In Buddhism, Sunyata ("Emptiness, illusory nature of phenomena, voidness, non-reality").

The ultimate nature of reality, which is impossible to convey in words. In Buddhist philosophy, it is described as paramarthasatya (ultimate truth), dharmata (actual reality), and tathata (suchness), each of which attempt to communicate the total absence of self-identity ("I") and inherent existence. Only through the experience of the voidness or emptiness can one understand it, and that experience can only be reached through a very specific type of meditation.

"Transcendent wisdom is inexpressible and inconceivable. Unborn and unceasing, it has the nature of space; It is realized through an individual's discernment And is the object of pristine awareness. It is the mother of all Buddhas throughout the three periods of time." –Buddha Shakyamuni

"Only in the absence of the ego can we directly experience Illuminating Emptiness." –Samael Aun Weor, *The Mystery of the Golden Flower*

"Those who are ignorant of the void cannot achieve liberation. These confused minds wander in the prison of the six realms." –Bodhichittavivarana

Initiation: The process whereby the Innermost (the Inner Father) receives recognition, empowerment and greater responsibilities in the Internal Worlds, and little by little approaches His goal: complete Self-realization, or in other words, the return into the Absolute. Initiation NEVER applies to the "I" or our terrestrial personality.

"There are nine Initiations of Minor Mysteries and seven great Initiations of Major Mysteries. The INNERMOST is the one who receives all of these Initiations. The Testament of Wisdom says: "Before the dawning of the false aurora upon the earth, the ones who survived the hurricane and the tempest were praising the INNERMOST, and the heralds of the aurora appeared unto them." The psychological "I" does not receives Initiations. The human personality does not receive anything. Nonetheless, the "I" of some Initiates becomes filled with pride when saying 'I am a Master, I have such Initiations.' Thus, this is how the "I" believes itself to be an Initiate and keeps reincarnating in order to "perfect itself", but, the "I" never ever perfects itself. The "I" only reincarnates in order to satisfy desires. That is all." –Samael Aun Weor, *The Aquarian Message*

Initiations of Major Mysteries: The qualifications of the consciousness as it ascends into greater degrees of wisdom. The first five Initiations of Major Mysteries correspond to the creation of the real Human Being. Learn more by studying these books by Samael Aun Weor: *The Perfect Matrimony, The Three Mountains,* and *The Revolution of Beelzebub.*

"High initiation is the fusion of two principles: Atman-Buddhi, through the five principal Initiations of Major Mysteries. With the first we achieve the fusion of Atman-Buddhi, and with the fifth, we add the Manas to this fusion, and so the septenary is reduced to a trinity: "Atman-Buddhi Manas." There are a total of Nine Initiations of Major Mysteries." –Samael Aun Weor, *The Zodiacal Course*

"We fulfill our human evolution with the five Initiations of Major Mysteries. The remaining three Initiations and the degree of "Lord of the World" are of a "Super-Human" nature." –Samael Aun Weor, *Esoteric Medicine and Practical Magic*

Innermost: "Our real Being is of a universal nature. Our real Being is neither a kind of superior nor inferior "I." Our real Being is impersonal, universal, divine. He transcends every concept of "I," me, myself, ego, etc., etc." –Samael Aun Weor, *The Perfect Matrimony*

Also known as Atman, the Spirit, Chesed, our own individual interior divine Father.

"The Innermost is the ardent flame of Horeb. In accordance with Moses, the Innermost is the Ruach Elohim (the Spirit of God) who sowed the waters in the beginning of the world. He is the Sun King, our Divine

Monad, the Alter-Ego of Cicerone." —Samael Aun Weor, *The Revolution of Beelzebub*

Intellectual Animal: The current state of humanity: animals with intellect.

When the Intelligent Principle, the Monad, sends its spark of consciousness into Nature, that spark, the anima, enters into manifestation as a simple mineral. Gradually, over millions of years, the anima gathers experience and evolves up the chain of life until it perfects itself in the level of the mineral kingdom. It then graduates into the plant kingdom, and subsequently into the animal kingdom. With each ascension the spark receives new capacities and higher grades of complexity. In the animal kingdom it learns procreation by ejaculation. When that animal intelligence enters into the human kingdom, it receives a new capacity: reasoning, the intellect; it is now an anima with intellect: an Intellectual Animal. That spark must then perfect itself in the human kingdom in order to become a complete and perfect human being, an entity that has conquered and transcended everything that belongs to the lower kingdoms. Unfortunately, very few intellectual animals perfect themselves; most remain enslaved by their animal nature, and thus are reabsorbed by Nature, a process belonging to the devolving side of life and called by all the great religions "Hell" or the Second Death.

"The present manlike being is not yet human; he is merely an intellectual animal. It is a very grave error to call the legion of the "I" the "soul." In fact, what the manlike being has is the psychic material, the material for the soul within his Essence, but indeed, he does not have a Soul yet." —Samael Aun Weor, *The Revolution of the Dialectic*

Internal Worlds: The many dimensions beyond the physical world. These dimensions are both subjective and objective. To know the objective internal worlds (the astral plane, or Nirvana, or the Klipoth) one must first know one's own personal, subjective internal worlds, because the two are intimately associated.

"Whosoever truly wants to know the internal worlds of the planet Earth or of the solar system or of the galaxy in which we live, must previously know his intimate world, his individual, internal life, his own internal worlds. Man, know thyself, and thou wilt know the universe and its gods. The more we explore this internal world called "myself," the more we will comprehend that we simultaneously live in two worlds, in two realities, in two confines: the external and the internal. In the same way that it is indispensable for one to learn how to walk in the external world so as not to fall down into a precipice, or not get lost in the streets of the city, or to select one's friends, or not associate with the perverse ones, or not eat poison, etc.; likewise, through the psychological work upon oneself we learn how to walk in the internal world, which is explorable only through Self-observation." —Samael Aun Weor, *Treatise of Revolutionary Psychology*

Through the work in Self-observation, we develop the capacity to awaken where previously we were asleep: including in the objective internal worlds.

Karma: (Sanskrit, literally "deed"; derived from kri, "to do...") The law of cause and effect.

"Be not deceived; God is not mocked: for whatsoever a man soweth, that shall he also reap." –Galatians 6:7

Kundabuffer: Originally a useful organ that served the function of helping ancient humanity become focused on material, physical existence, it became corrupted by desire and sexual fall, thus resulting in the emergence of the ego and the fortification of the sexual energy in a negative polarity, and has since been symbolized by the tail of the devils, the tail of Satan.

"It is necessary to know that the Kundabuffer organ is the negative development of the fire. This is the descending serpent, which precipitates itself from the coccyx downwards, towards the atomic infernos of the human being. The Kundabuffer organ is the horrifying tail of Satan, which is shown in the "body of desires" of the intellectual animal, who in the present times is falsely called human." –Samael Aun Weor, *The Elimination of Satan's Tail*

"The diabolic type whose seduction is here, there and everywhere under the pretext of working in the Ninth Sphere, who abandons his wife because he thinks she will not be useful to him for the work in the fiery forge of Vulcan, instead of awakening Kundalini, will awaken the abominable Kundabuffer organ. A certain Initiate, whose name will not be mentioned in this treatise, commits the error of attributing to the Kundalini all the sinister qualities of the Kundabuffer organ... When the Fire is cast downwards from the chakra of the coccyx, the tail of Satan appears; the abominable Kundabuffer organ. The hypnotic power of the organ of Witches' Sabbath holds the human multitude asleep and depraved. Those who commit the crime of practicing Black Tantra (Sexual Magic with seminal ejaculation) clearly awaken and develop the organ of all fatalities. Those who betray their guru or master, even if practicing White Tantra (without seminal ejaculation), will obviously activate the organ of all evils. Such sinister power opens the seven doorways of the lower abdomen (the seven infernal chakras) and converts us into terribly perverse demons." –Samael Aun Weor, *The Secret of the Golden Flower*

Kundalini: "Kundalini, the serpent power or mystic fire, is the primordial energy or Sakti that lies dormant or sleeping in the Muladhara Chakra, the centre of the body. It is called the serpentine or annular power on account of serpentine form. It is an electric fiery occult power, the great pristine force which underlies all organic and inorganic matter. Kundalini is the cosmic power in individual bodies. It is not a material force like electricity, magnetism, centripetal or centrifugal force. It is a spiritual potential Sakti or cosmic power. In reality it has no form. [...] O Divine Mother Kundalini, the Divine Cosmic Energy that is hidden in men!

Thou art Kali, Durga, Adisakti, Rajarajeswari, Tripurasundari, Maha-Lakshmi, Maha-Sarasvati! Thou hast put on all these names and forms. Thou hast manifested as Prana, electricity, force, magnetism, cohesion, gravitation in this universe. This whole universe rests in Thy bosom. Crores of salutations unto thee. O Mother of this world! Lead me on to open the Sushumna Nadi and take Thee along the Chakras to Sahasrara Chakra and to merge myself in Thee and Thy consort, Lord Siva. Kundalini Yoga is that Yoga which treats of Kundalini Sakti, the six centres of spiritual energy (Shat Chakras), the arousing of the sleeping Kundalini Sakti and its union with Lord Siva in Sahasrara Chakra, at the crown of the head. This is an exact science. This is also known as Laya Yoga. The six centres are pierced (Chakra Bheda) by the passing of Kundalini Sakti to the top of the head. 'Kundala' means 'coiled'. Her form is like a coiled serpent. Hence the name Kundalini." –Swami Sivananda, *Kundalini Yoga*

"Kundalini is a compound word: Kunda reminds us of the abominable "Kundabuffer organ," and lini is an Atlantean term meaning termination. Kundalini means "the termination of the abominable Kundabuffer organ." In this case, it is imperative not to confuse Kundalini with Kundabuffer." –Samael Aun Weor, *The Great Rebellion*

These two forces, one positive and ascending, and one negative and descending, are symbolized in the Bible in the book of Numbers (the story of the serpent of brass). The Kundalini is "The power of life."- from the Theosophical Glossary. The sexual fire that is at the base of all life.

"The ascent of the Kundalini along the spinal cord is achieved very slowly in accordance with the merits of the heart. The fires of the heart control the miraculous development of the sacred serpent. Devi Kundalini is not something mechanical as many suppose; the igneous serpent is only awakened with genuine Love between husband and wife, and it will never rise up along the medullar canal of adulterers." –Samael Aun Weor, *The Secret of the Golden Flower*

"The decisive factor in the progress, development and evolution of the Kundalini is ethics." –Samael Aun Weor, *The Revolution of Beelzebub*

"Until not too long ago, the majority of spiritualists believed that on awakening the Kundalini, the latter instantaneously rose to the head and the initiate was automatically united with his Innermost or Internal God, instantly, and converted into Mahatma. How comfortable! How comfortably all these theosophists, Rosicrucians and spiritualists, etc., imagined High Initiation." –Samael Aun Weor, *The Zodiacal Course*

"There are seven bodies of the Being. Each body has its "cerebrospinal" nervous system, its medulla and Kundalini. Each body is a complete organism. There are, therefore, seven bodies, seven medullae and seven Kundalinis. The ascension of each of the seven Kundalinis is slow and difficult. Each canyon or vertebra represents determined occult powers and this is why the conquest of each canyon undergoes terrible tests." –Samael Aun Weor, *The Zodiacal Course*

Logos: (Greek, plural Logoi) means Verb or Word. In Greek and Hebrew metaphysics, the unifying principle of the world. The Logos is the manifested deity of every nation and people; the outward expression or the effect of the cause which is ever concealed. (Speech is the "logos" of thought). The Logos has three aspects, known universally as the Trinity or Trimurti. The First Logos is the Father, Brahma. The Second Logos is the Son, Vishnu. The Third Logos is the Holy Spirit, Shiva. One who incarnates the Logos becomes a Logos.

"The Logos is not an individual. The Logos is an army of ineffable beings." —Samael Aun Weor, *Sexology, the Basis of Endocrinology and Criminology*

Lumisial: "A place of light." A Gnostic Lumisial is a generator of spiritual energy, a Gnostic school which maintains the ancient initiatic Three Chamber structure. The source of power is the Cosmic Christ, and the means to receive and transform it are within the Second and Third Chambers.

"We are therefore working, my dear brethren, to initiate the Era of Aquarius. We are working in order to save what is possible, meaning, those who allow themselves to be saved. This is why it is necessary that we shape our Gnostic Movements and that we organize them each time better; that we establish the Three Chambers. Our Gnostic Movements must have exactly Three Chambers. Each Lumisial must have Three Chambers for the instruction of our students. Our Gnostic Centers receive a name in a very pure language that flows like a river of gold that runs in the sunny, thick jungle; that name is LUMISIALS." - Samael Aun Weor, *The Final Catastrophe and the Extraterrestrials*

Magic: The word magic is derived from the ancient word "mag" that means priest. Real magic is the work of a priest. A real magician is a priest.

"Magic, according to Novalis, is the art of influencing the inner world consciously." —Samael Aun Weor, *The Secret of the Golden Flower*

"When magic is explained as it really is, it seems to make no sense to fanatical people. They prefer to follow their world of illusions." —Samael Aun Weor, *The Revolution of Beelzebub*

Master: Like many terms related to spirituality, this one is grossly misunderstood. Although many people claim to be "masters," the truth is that the terrestrial person is only a terrestrial person. The only one who can be a master is the Innermost, Atman, the Father, Chesed.

"And, behold, one came and said unto [Jesus], Good master, what good thing shall I do, that I may have eternal life? And he said unto him, Why callest thou me good? there is none good but one, that is, God." —Matthew 19

"The value of the human person which is the intellectual animal called human being is less than the ash of a cigarette. However, the fools feel themselves to be giants. Unfortunately, within all the pseudo-esoteric currents a great amount of mythomaniac people exist, individuals who feel themselves to be masters, people who enjoy when others call them masters, individuals who believe themselves to be Gods, individuals who presume to be saints. The only one who is truly great is the Spirit, the Innermost. We, the intellectual animals, are leaves that the wind tosses about... No student of occultism is a master. True masters are only those who have reached the Fifth Initiation of Major Mysteries [Tiphereth, the causal body]. Before the Fifth Initiation nobody is a master." —Samael Aun Weor, *The Perfect Matrimony*

"You [if you have reached levels of initiation] are not the master, you are only the sinning shadow of He who has never sinned. Remember that only your internal Lamb is the master. Remember that even though your internal God is a Hierarch of fire, you, poor slug, are only a human being and as a human being you will always be judged. Your internal Lamb could be a planetary God, but you, poor slug of the mud, do not forget, always remember that you are only the shadow of your God. Poor sinning shadow..! Do not say "I am this God" or "I am that master," because you are only a shadow that must resolve to die and be slaughtered in order not to serve as an obstacle for your internal God. It is necessary for you to reach supreme humbleness." —Samael Aun Weor, *The Aquarian Message*

"Do not accept external masters in the physical plane. Learn how to travel in the astral body, and when you are skillful in the astral, choose an authentic master of Major Mysteries of the White Brotherhood and consecrate unto him the most absolute devotion and the most profound respect." —Samael Aun Weor, *The Zodiacal Course*

Meditation: "When the esotericist submerges himself into meditation, what he seeks is information." —Samael Aun Weor

"It is urgent to know how to meditate in order to comprehend any psychic aggregate, or in other words, any psychological defect. It is indispensable to know how to work with all our heart and with all our soul, if we want the elimination to occur." —Samael Aun Weor, *The Gnostic Bible: The Pistis Sophia Unveiled*

"1. The Gnostic must first attain the ability to stop the course of his thoughts, the capacity to not think. Indeed, only the one who achieves that capacity will hear the Voice of the Silence.

"2. When the Gnostic disciple attains the capacity to not think, then he must learn to concentrate his thoughts on only one thing.

"3. The third step is correct meditation. This brings the first flashes of the new consciousness into the mind.

"4. The fourth step is contemplation, ecstasy or Samadhi. This is the state of Turiya (perfect clairvoyance)." —Samael Aun Weor, *The Perfect Matrimony*

Nirvana: (Sanskrit, "extinction" or "cessation"; Tibetan: nyangde, literally "the state beyond sorrow") In general use, refers to the permanent cessation of suffering and its causes, and therefore refers to a state of consciousness rather than a place. Yet, the term can also apply to heavenly realms, whose vibration is directed related to the cessation of suffering. In other words, if your mind-stream has liberated itself from the causes of suffering, it will naturally vibrate at the level of Nirvana (heaven).

"When the Soul fuses with the Inner Master, then it becomes free from Nature and enters into the supreme happiness of absolute existence. This state of happiness is called Nirvana. Nirvana can be attained through millions of births and deaths, but it can also be attained by means of a shorter path; this is the path of "initiation." The Initiate can reach Nirvana in one single life if he so wants it." –Samael Aun Weor, *The Zodiacal Course*

Root Races: "Every planet develops seven root races and seven subraces. Our planet Earth already developed five root races; it needs to develop two more root races. After the seven root races, the planet Earth, already transformed by cataclysms over the course of millions of years, will become a new moon." –Samael Aun Weor, *The Kabbalah of the Mayan Mysteries*

The seven root races of this planet Earth are:

1. Polar protoplasmatic
2. Hyperborean
3. Lemurian
4. Atlantean
5. Aryan (present)
6. Koradi (future)
7. (Seventh) (future)

Furthermore, each root race has seven subraces.

Samsara: (Sanskrit; Tibetan khorwa) Cyclic, conditioned existence whose defining characteristic is suffering. It is contrasted with nirvana.

Self-realization: The achievement of perfect knowledge. This phrase is better stated as, "The realization of the Innermost Self," or "The realization of the true nature of self." At the ultimate level, this is the experiential, conscious knowledge of the Absolute, which is synonymous with Emptiness, Shunyata, or Non-being.

Sexual Magic: The word magic is derived from the ancient word magos "one of the members of the learned and priestly class," from O.Pers. magush, possibly from PIE *magh- "to be able, to have power." [Quoted from Online Etymology Dictionary].

"All of us possess some electrical and magnetic forces within, and, just like a magnet, we exert a force of attraction and repulsion... Between lovers that magnetic force is particularly powerful and its action has a far-reaching effect." –Samael Aun Weor, *The Secret of the Golden Flower*

Sexual magic refers to an ancient science that has been known and protected by the purest, most spiritually advanced human beings, whose purpose and goal is the harnessing and perfection of our sexual forces. A more accurate translation of sexual magic would be "sexual priesthood." In ancient times, the priest was always accompanied by a priestess, for they represent the divine forces at the base of all creation: the masculine and feminine, the Yab-Yum, Ying-Yang, Father-Mother: the Elohim. Unfortunately, the term "sexual magic" has been grossly misinterpreted by mistaken persons such as Aleister Crowley, who advocated a host of degenerated practices, all of which belong solely to the lowest and most perverse mentality and lead only to the enslavement of the consciousness, the worship of lust and desire, and the decay of humanity. True, upright, heavenly sexual magic is the natural harnessing of our latent forces, making them active and harmonious with nature and the divine, and which leads to the perfection of the human being.

"People are filled with horror when they hear about sexual magic; however, they are not filled with horror when they give themselves to all kinds of sexual perversion and to all kinds of carnal passion." –Samael Aun Weor, *The Perfect Matrimony*

Solar Bodies: The physical, vital, astral, mental, and causal bodies that are created through the beginning stages of alchemy/tantra and that provide a basis for existence in their corresponding levels of nature, just as the physical body does in the physical world. These bodies or vehicles are superior due to being created out of solar (Christic) energy, as opposed to the inferior, lunar bodies we receive from nature. Also known as the Wedding Garment (Christianity), the Merkabah (Kabbalah), To Soma Heliakon (Greek), and Sahu (Egyptian).

"All the masters of the White Lodge, the angels, archangels, thrones, seraphim, virtues, etc. are garbed with the solar bodies. Only those who have solar bodies have the Being incarnated. Only someone who possesses the Being is an authentic human being." –Samael Aun Weor, *The Esoteric Treatise of Hermetic Astrology*

Subjective: "What do modern psychologists understand as 'objective?' They understand it to be that which is external to the mind: the physical, the tangible, the material.

"Yet, they are totally mistaken, because when analysing the term "subjective," we see that it signifies "sub, under," that which is below the range of our perceptions. What is below our perceptions? Is it not perhaps the Infernal Worlds? Is it not perhaps subjective that which is in the physical or beneath the physical? So, what is truly subjective is what is below the limits of our perceptions.

"Psychologists do not know how to use the former terms correctly.

"Objective: the light, the resplendence; it is that which contains the Truth, clarity, lucidity.

"Subjective: the darkness, the tenebrous. The subjective elements of perception are the outcome of seeing, hearing, touching, smelling and tasting. All of these are perceptions of what we see in the third dimension. For example, in one cube we see only length, width and height. We do not see the fourth dimension because we are bottled up within the ego. The subjective elements of perception are constituted by the ego with all of its "I's." —Samael Aun Weor, *Tarot and Kabbalah*

Tantra: Sanskrit for "continuum" or "unbroken stream." This refers first (1) to the continuum of vital energy that sustains all existence, and second (2) to the class of knowledge and practices that harnesses that vital energy, thereby transforming the practitioner. There are many schools of Tantra, but they can be classified in three types: White, Grey and Black. Tantra has long been known in the West as Alchemy.

"In the view of Tantra, the body's vital energies are the vehicles of the mind. When the vital energies are pure and subtle, one's state of mind will be accordingly affected. By transforming these bodily energies we transform the state of consciousness." —The 14th Dalai Lama

Tree of Life: (Hebrew) Although the Hebrew term is plural ("Tree of Lives") it is usually rendered singular.

"And out of the ground made the LORD God to grow every tree that is pleasant to the sight, and good for food; the tree of life also in the midst of the garden, and the tree of knowledge of good and evil." —Genesis 2:9

This tree represents the structure of the soul (microcosm) and of the universe (macrocosm).

"The Tree of Life is the spinal medulla. This tree of wisdom is also the ten sephiroth, the twenty-two creative Major Arcana, letters, sounds and numbers, with which the Logos (God) created the universe." —from Alcione, a lecture by Samael Aun Weor

White Lodge or Brotherhood: That ancient collection of pure souls who maintain the highest and most sacred of sciences: White Magic or White Tantra. It is called White due to its purity and cleanliness. This "Brotherhood" or "Lodge" includes human beings of the highest order from every race, culture, creed and religion, and of both sexes.

Yoga: (Sanskrit) "union." Similar to the Latin "religare," the root of the word "religion." In Tibetan, it is "rnal-'byor" which means "union with the fundamental nature of reality."

"The word YOGA comes from the root Yuj which means to join, and in its spiritual sense, it is that process by which the human spirit is brought into near and conscious communion with, or is merged in, the Divine Spirit, according as the nature of the human spirit is held to be separate from (Dvaita, Visishtadvaita) or one with (Advaita) the Divine Spirit." —Swami Sivananda, *Kundalini Yoga*

"Patanjali defines Yoga as the suspension of all the functions of the mind. As such, any book on Yoga, which does not deal with these three aspects of the subject, viz., mind, its functions and the method of suspending them, can he safely laid aside as unreliable and incomplete." —Swami Sivananda, *Practical Lessons In Yoga*

"The word yoga means in general to join one's mind with an actual fact..." —The 14th Dalai Lama

"The soul aspires for the union with his Innermost, and the Innermost aspires for the union with his Glorian." —Samael Aun Weor, *The Revolution of Beelzebub*

"Yoga does not consist in sitting cross-legged for six hours or stopping the beatings of the heart or getting oneself buried underneath the ground for a week or a month. These are all physical feats only. Yoga is the science that teaches you the method of uniting the individual will with the Cosmic Will. Yoga transmutes the unregenerate nature and increases energy, vitality, vigour, and bestows longevity and a high standard of health." —Swami Sivananda, *Autobiography*

"Brahmacharya [sexual purity] is the very foundation of Yoga." —Swami Sivananda

"The Yoga that we require today is actually ancient Gnostic Christian Yoga, which absolutely rejects the idea of Hatha Yoga. We do not recommend Hatha Yoga simply because, spiritually speaking, the acrobatics of this discipline are fruitless; they should be left to the acrobats of the circus." —Samael Aun Weor, *The Yellow Book*

"Yoga has been taught very badly in the Western world. Multitudes of pseudo-sapient Yogis have spread the false belief that the true Yogi must be an infrasexual (an enemy of sex). Some of these false yogis have never even visited India; they are infrasexual pseudo-yogis. These ignoramuses believe that they are going to achieve in-depth realization only with the yogic exercises, such as asanas, pranayamas, etc. Not only do they have such false beliefs, but what is worse is that they propagate them; thus, they misguide many people away from the difficult, straight, and narrow door that leads unto the light. No authentically initiated Yogi from India would ever think that he could achieve his inner self-realization with pranayamas or asanas, etc. Any legitimate Yogi from India knows very well that such yogic exercises are only co-assistants that are very useful for their health and for the development of their powers, etc. Only the Westerners and pseudo-yogis have within their minds the belief that they can achieve Self-realization with such exercises. Sexual Magic is practiced very secretly within the Ashrams of India. Any true yogi initiate from India works with the Arcanum A.Z.F. This is taught by the great Yogis from India that have visited the Western world, and if it has not been taught by these great, initiated Hindustani Yogis, if it has not been published in their books of Yoga, it was in order to avoid scandals. You can be absolutely sure that the Yogis who do not practice Sexual Magic will never achieve birth in the superior worlds. Thus, whosoever affirms the contrary is a liar, an impostor." —Samael Aun Weor, *Alchemy and Kabbalah in the Tarot*

Index

About the Author

His name is Hebrew סמאל און ואור, and is pronounced "samayel on vay-or." You may not have heard of him, but Samael Aun Weor changed the world.

In 1950, in his first two books, he became the first person to reveal the esoteric secret hidden in all the world's great religions, and for that, accused of "healing the ill," he was put in prison. Nevertheless, he did not stop. Between 1950 and 1977 – merely twenty-seven years – not only did Samael Aun Weor write over sixty books on the most difficult subjects in the world, such as consciousness, kabbalah, physics, tantra, meditation, etc., in which he deftly exposed the singular root of all knowledge – which he called Gnosis – he simultaneously inspired millions of people across the entire span of Latin America: stretching across twenty countries and an area of more than 21,000,000 square kilometers, founding schools everywhere, even in places without electricity or post offices.

During those twenty-seven years, he experienced all the extremes that humanity could give him, from adoration to death threats, and in spite of the enormous popularity of his books and lectures, he renounced an income, refused recognitions, walked away from accolades, and consistently turned away those who would worship him. He held as friends both presidents and peasants, and yet remained a mystery to all.

When one reflects on the effort and will it requires to perform even day to day tasks, it is astonishing to consider the herculean efforts required to accomplish what he did in such a short time. But, there is a reason: he was a man who knew who he was, and what he had to do. A true example of compassion and selfless service, Samael Aun Weor dedicated the whole of his life to freely helping anyone and everyone find the path out of suffering. His mission was to show all of humanity the universal source of all spiritual traditions, which he did not only through his writings and lectures, but also through his actions. He said,

> "I, the one who writes this book, am not anyone's master, and I beg people to not follow me. I am an imperfect human just like anyone else, and it is an error to follow someone who is imperfect. Let every one follow their "I am [their Innermost]...
>
> "I do not want to receive visitors. Unquestionably, I am nothing more than a postman, a courier, a man that delivers a message... It would be the breaking point of silliness for you to come from your country to the capital city of Mexico with the only purpose of visiting a vulgar postman, an employee that delivered you a letter in the past... Why would you waste your money for that? Why would you visit a simple courier, a miserable postman? It is better for you to study the message, the written teachings delivered in the books...
>
> "I have not come to form any sect, or one more belief, nor am I interested in the schools of today, or the particular beliefs of anyone! ...
>
> "We are not interested in anyone's money, nor are we interested in monthly fees, or temples made out of brick, cement or clay, because we are conscious visitors in the cathedral of the soul and we know that wisdom is of the soul.
>
> "Flattery tires us, praise should only belong to our Father (who is in secret and watches over us minutely).
>
> "We are not in search of followers; all we want is for each person to follow his or her self–their own internal master, their sacred Innermost–because he is the only one who can save and glorify us.
>
> "I do not follow anyone, therefore no one should follow me...

"We do not want any more comedies, pretenses, false mysticism, or false schools. What we want now are living realities; we want to prepare ourselves to see, hear, and touch the reality of those truths..." –Samael Aun Weor

Your book reviews matter.

Glorian Publishing is a very small non-profit organization, thus we have no money to spend on marketing and advertising. Fortunately, there is a proven way to gain the attention of readers: book reviews. Mainstream book reviewers won't review these books, but you can.

The path of liberation requires the daily balance of three active factors:

- birth of virtue
- death of vice
- sacrifice for others

Writing book reviews is a powerful way to sacrifice for others. By writing book reviews on popular websites, you help to make the books more visible to humanity, and you might help save a soul from suffering. Will you do your part to help us show these wonderful teachings to others? Take a moment today to write a review.

Donate

Glorian Publishing is a non-profit publisher dedicated to spreading the sacred universal doctrine to suffering humanity. All of our works are made possible by the kindness and generosity of sponsors. If you would like to make a tax-deductible donation, you may send it to the address below, or visit our website for other alternatives. If you would like to sponsor the publication of a book, please contact us at (844) 945-6742 or help@glorian.org.

Glorian Publishing
PO Box 209
Clinton, CT 06413 US
Phone: (844) 945-6742

VISIT US ONLINE AT glorian.org